World Banking World **Fraud**

USING YOUR IDENTITY

John Cruz

ISBN: 146378659X
ISBN-13: 9781463786595
Library of Congress Control Number: 2011913782
CreateSpace, North Charleston, SC

shang·haied shang·hai·ing
Definition of SHANGHAI
transitive verb

1   **a :** to put aboard a ship by force often with
     the help of liquor or a drug
     b : to put by force or threat of force into or as if
     into a place of detention
2   **a:** to put by trickery into an undesirable position

Merriam-Webster, Online Dictionary

This is a true story. Only the names have been changed to protect the innocent.

Introduction

I had only held this position for a little over a month, and it was already a nightmare.

When I worked in Nassau County as the vice president of the local Long Island Federal Credit Union, I had my own book of clients. I knew the clients and they knew me. Business was good. I liked to keep it simple. Customers respect that. But now I was covering all of Long Island for HSBC, and I was cleaning up the mess the last branch manager had made of things. And since she had simply disappeared from the job after meeting with security one afternoon a few weeks ago, my task was even more burdensome.

Making loans should be simple. Anyone who's heard of the subprime mortgage crisis can understand that when you start to creatively lend money, you at the same time take unnecessary risk. And risk leads to default. For all the mysticism and technical jargon about money and moneylending, the truth is simple and comes down to one question: if it were your money, who would you lend it to?

Now, that can be a tough question to answer as well, which is why banks, and HSBC is no exception, have procedures and criteria to follow. These procedures may seem harsh when you're sitting across from a lender who's saying no, but if it were your money and your business to lose, you'd be careful how you lent it out and who you lent it to. It probably also goes without saying that if you ran a bank, you'd keep away from customers without tax returns or those with fake names, social security numbers, and tax IDs. But from what I could gather, HSBC—and particularly the last branch manager of East Northport—had an attraction to just that sort of client. This wouldn't have been so bad—well, it would have, but the situation was made worse by the fact that it was also now my responsibility to maintain and increase the numbers this branch produced. Cutting out the sort of fraud and money laundering I had begun finding would cut into the bottom line, which would not only hurt my compensation but would turn the higher-ups against me.

When you take a job like this at a major financial institution, you hardly ever think it will entail turning a blind eye to criminal behavior. At least I didn't when I signed on at HSBC a little over a year before. Back then, life was good. I wasn't implicated in banking fraud and money laundering. Of course, that was before the new segment leader decided to put me in charge as the senior business relationship manager over some of the highest-producing branches in the country. Little did I know that their performance got a big bump from phantom businesses that had apparently made only seven thousand dollars a year ago but just last week had had three million go in and out of their checking accounts in small amounts of twenty, forty and sixty K from PayPal. I guess apparently they operated with a very low profit margin; either that or they increased business by some 20,000 percent this year.

Unfortunately, there wasn't only one account like this one; there were hundreds. Every week that passed brought only more creative accounting, which made it only more apparent that this was something I couldn't turn a blind eye to. But it was about to get worse.

While uncovering new and ever more inventive ways the bank assisted money laundering was exciting, I was also expected to periodically verify that the businesses we lent money to and had accounts with really were who they said they were. So I was out on the Long Island Expressway headed east. My first stop was a small insurance company called S&S, whose phone number turned out to be disconnected and whose tax ID number actually corresponded with another customer from Yonkers who had recently closed their account with HSBC. This was alarming, of course, and when I had worked detecting fraud for the local credit union, there would have been other people at the bank who also thought this was alarming. But at such a large corporation like the Hong Kong and Shanghai Banking Corporation, this type of behavior was hardly worth looking into.

Nevertheless, here I was. I had driven out this way to meet with the manager of another branch I oversaw, and so I figured I would stop in, just to be sure. Mistakes do happen, of course, and I'd like to say that I was expecting to pull up and find the business fully operational. But after six weeks or so in my new duties, I had already lost that kind of innocence and naiveté.

Just as I thought, when I pulled in to where the business should have sat near the Brentwood Station on the LIRR off Suffolk Avenue, the building turned out to be empty. It obviously hadn't been occupied in some time. A few windows were broken, and weeds pushed up through the gray concrete. But maybe the address was incorrect. I looked down at the laptop on the passenger seat beside me. The documents flickered on the screen. No. I had the right address. The business didn't exist.

As someone who used to work at a place where I not only knew everyone by name but nearly every client we dealt with, I was under the impression that companies operated by their books and within the law. And that people, though they can and do lie, are generally honest, save for the few bad apples. I had never seen a "culture of corruption" before. But I was about to get firsthand experience of what that type of culture can do, especially when it's part of a multinational, multi-billion-dollar company hell bent on protecting itself at every turn.

In the parking lot, I glanced back through the files I had brought with me on the computer. I was eating my lunch, and I looked down to double check and see

Index of abandoned addresses!

that I was right in what I had found. After all, since I had begun to hand in the more major instances of fraud I encountered, I had been getting pushback from corporate. But as I looked a little more closely at the documents, I noticed something that went beyond what I had so far seen at this company. I saw that the last loan this dummy company received actually had my name on it. Somehow my stamp was used to notarize that this company's paperwork was as it should be so it could receive a loan. *≠ notary function*

I dropped the laptop back onto the seat beside me, and leaned back. I felt betrayed, and I felt stupid. My move to HSBC was one of the largest in my career, though not as large as my jump from a farm upstate to the armed forces and college. Nevertheless, when I left the old credit union for this multinational, I more than doubled my salary. Even the benefits were better, and it seemed like just a matter of time before I moved up the ladder as I had moved up every other ladder. And this was exactly what I didn't want: to be enmeshed in corruption and fraud. The fact that my name was used angered me even more.

I am not a crusader. I got into banking so I could make money. And I moved to HSBC so I could make more money. This sort of discovery would be bad business for everyone involved. But it was my job to fix this problem and send the information up the corporate chain of command so we could straighten this thing out. Even at this point, and though I had already encountered flak for discovering fraud, I believed the company would stand behind me. After all, I was an honest employee whose identity had just been used to help give a straw company a loan. How could they expect me to allow that to happen? It meant that my region would lose money this month and possibly for the entire quarter, but after we took that hit, I was certain I could turn it around. After all, my first year at HSBC, when I was still at the Carle Place branch and before moving here, I was the number one producing manager in the region.

I stepped out of the car that afternoon not only ready to defend my claims but also with a rehearsed plan to make back what we would be losing. The only thing I wasn't ready for was first to be ignored and then to be discredited and ultimately fired. The truth can be a funny thing sometimes, especially when everyone else either doesn't believe that the truth matters or is determined to see that the facts never see the light of day. And when you have two agendas so diametrically opposed to each other, as was my personal obligation against the corporate agenda, only one side will win.

Chapter 1

I know firsthand what it's like to work your way up from the bottom. And what it's like to achieve the American dream only to be crushed by a multinational, simply because you won't allow it and its unscrupulous employees to use your identity to commit fraud and money laundering. I don't know whose money was really being laundered—if I knew that I would probably be dead—but I do have firsthand knowledge and proof of how the Hong Kong and Shanghai Banking Corporation helped launder and circulate nearly a billion dollars through accounts linked to companies that did not exist. And how this process was facilitated not just by managers at the branch level but also by segment leaders, and by executives on at least the regional level of the corporation, which may not sound high up the chain until you consider that the region I was in was southern New York, which accounts for some 50 percent of the bank's North American business.

I had worked my entire life to earn the position I held, and now I was surrounded by the worst sort of crooks. The fact that the fraud was so blatant meant that anyone in the company with eyes knew what was going on. On top of the open fraud, it made no sense for me to have been moved to Suffolk County and parts of Manhattan (geographically skipping over Nassau County) when I had just brought my own clients to HSBC from the Long Island Federal Credit Union in Carle Place, Nassau County. Further still, since I had moved to the HSBC branch location in Carle Place, I had only expanded the client base that I had brought with me. Moving me was pointless.

Now I was placed over a widespread group of Long Island branches because the new segment leader got it into his head that it was a good management tactic to shake things up. What he could never have intended was exactly how badly things were about to get shaken up—an eventuality that would only bring him to try and ruin me rather than admit that the bank's performance and adherence to its own policies as well as to government regulations left much to be desired. The shake-up would finally result in his demotion, followed by my termination, and then, within a year, the discreet jettisoning of most of HSBC's senior executives for the entire region.

It might be hard to believe now, but I didn't want to deal with the fraud when I first began to discover it. I didn't care about it. I found it. I reported it, but it was someone else's job to fix it. It was my job to do business, and I wanted to build new clients and make more money; as I said, that's why I decided to move to HSBC in the first place. I wanted to be the "trusted advisor"—"the businessman's banker." But pretty soon I couldn't stomach the outright and disgusting level of fraud I found, from bad loans to straw companies with fake addresses and fake tax ID numbers on business accounts. Couple these findings, and more, with the duplication and use of my own notary stamp, and I could no longer just stand pat and treat my day-to-day activities as business as usual. I hadn't signed on for this, but I also wasn't going to put up with it either.

I had loved my job at the Long Island Federal Credit Union. There I felt like I was actually helping business owners. The old movie *It's a Wonderful Life* may be a bit cheesy, but there is still a part of everyone that hopes that this type of wholesomeness is really alive in the world. I didn't actually imagine myself as the third Baily brother at the "Building and Loan," but I did believe in helping the honest working stiffs. I still held the belief that the local banker may really be a kind and decent human being who is looking out for the best interests of the community. Jokes about Fannie and Freddie aside, I liked to think that this was what I did. I know it sounds a little contrived, but the idea that there really is good in the world is so much more comforting to believe in than what I had endured as a boy. It's not that I had a rough childhood—I didn't have a childhood. I worked my way through darkness to just a sliver of light, and I clung to that light and to the belief that it does get brighter for those who are upstanding and hardworking, because for me it had.

I was born in Brooklyn at King's County Hospital. My father left the family before I was five, so I have only the dimmest memory of him. What kind of memories do we really have when we're children? The answer to that is that it's often the horrific ones. And so the event that I do remember is when he hit my mother. I remember him shouting, and my little brother whimpering, and I remember that his fist was clenched when he did it.

That's a specific memory. I know it happened. But then he was gone, and my mother worked to raise the four of us on her own. He ran away and never came back—not even to attend her funeral. After having my own beautiful children, I've often wondered how a father can hurt his own and then run away. How could he just walk away as if he had no responsibility? And in my own little kid's mind, I started to question whether or not it was somehow my fault, and my doing that caused him to go.

My mother told us we were a burden to him, and that he just couldn't take it. When he moved out, we all had to move out also. We moved to a few different apartments before moving in with Dominick. Dominick was my mom's new husband. He wasn't so bad. I mean, he didn't beat us; he just didn't care for kids and so he ignored us, but being ignored was much better than being beaten. I also have an impression that he loved my mother and that he treated her well. But it wouldn't matter how well he treated her because it was all about to end. When I was six, my mother got pregnant with Dominick's baby. This should have been a moment for joy, but when she went to the doctor, she learned that she had cancer.

I was seven when she gave birth to my new little brother. My mom was so happy when she came home, but then her health took a turn for the worse. Dominick cared for her at our (his) apartment, but pretty soon it became too much for him to handle on his own, and he had to send her back to the hospital. She never left that hospital. She knew she was going to die.

The last time I saw her, she had something to tell me. She struggled to talk because to make words she had to hold her finger to the tube now coming from her throat. But I remember that she was adamant to talk to me. She said, "John, I'm dying. And when I die, things are going to be rough for you."

I'm sure I thought nothing as she spoke. How much could I possibly comprehend about what it would really mean for her to die and how permanent it would be? There was nothing for me to think because I was too young to know what those words would actually come to feel like. But even though I couldn't fully understand her then, what she went on to say has remained with me ever since, as if it were written in stone. There was a sense of urgency, and a sense that she wanted me to make a good life for myself, as she confided in me that day. She went on to tell me that there were two things I had to do in my life. The first was that I graduate from college. I can only wonder now what was going on in her mind: how she was looking at her seven-year-old boy and envisioning him growing into a teenager and then into a man. She clearly feared what I might become without a mother or father, growing up poor in Brooklyn. She said that no one in my family had ever gone to college before and that it was the only way that I could change my life for the better.

"Look at me," she said. "listen;" and then she gave me her final piece of wisdom:

"Get away from this family."

Chapter 2

When my mother died, she left behind five children. Our ages ranged between one and nine years old. She was only twenty-seven at the time. I had only known her for seven years, and I would never know her again, but what she told me never left me. At first it was impossible to enact her last wishes.

Dominick was gone shortly after my mother died. He took only his baby with him, and I never saw them again. The rest of us were sent to live with my grandparents in Moriches in southern, mid Suffolk County. It was mid-nowhere at the time. I have very little knowledge of how my grandparents came to live in Moriches. They were in their early forties then. They must have had my mother while they were still in their teens. No one ever told me that, though; there wasn't a lot of sharing about our family history. My grandparents mostly lived off welfare. However, my enterprising grandfather also had a side business outside of state-run entitlement programs.

The side business was actually a backyard business that consisted of a scrapyard/junkyard out back. The scrap was aligned in crooked rows with weeds and trees grown up around them. Along with the junk outside, the interior of the house was in shambles. There was dirt on the floors, and the bathroom was so filthy that even as a boy I preferred to go outside whenever I could. The house smelled because nothing was ever cleaned and because there were dead rats in the walls that my grandfather would shoot with his .22. He'd sit on the couch with the rifle propped on his knee listening for the rat's noise behind the old wainscoting. Then he'd take aim with his rifle where the sound was and fire. You usually knew the rats were dead when they screamed and then went silent. Sometimes they twitched in the wall for a while and then died. If he missed, he merely reloaded and fired again, leaving them dead in the walls with that smell permeating everything.

This is what he did when he wasn't sleeping, which was his favorite activity in life. My grandmother also shared his joy of sleeping. She always made it a point, though, to wake up in time to catch her favorite soaps on TV. When my grandfather woke up around noon, he'd go out for their breakfast, which consisted of coffee and a large bag of day-old doughnuts the shop was throwing away from the day before. He told the cook at the coffee shop that he fed them to the pigs, and so they held the doughnuts for him. In actuality, he fed us kids with the doughnuts first and threw the leftovers to the pigs. Eating day-old doughnuts was a treat compared to the dog food we were fed when things got really tight.

When I first moved in with them, my grandfather put me to work scrapping cars, which took up most of my time during school days. Now, I hardly ever went to school. Whenever I did, I got into fights. The other kids made fun of me because I was rarely bathed, I smelled, and my clothes all came from the Salvation Army, which made me an automatic target. I hated going to school. So working with the junk cars in the backyard was fine with me. I spent my time taking them apart and stacking the parts in separate piles. I took the seats out and stripped the cars to bare metal, or took the engines apart.

The scrapyard at my house became my refuge. It was full of broken toys that I got to play with. There were even cars that ran. I drove those around and created my own racecourse through the lanes and around the different piles of trash. I crashed the cars whenever I felt like it; after all, they were junk. And though some of them were nearly brand new, they were slated to be junked so whatever I did with them was fine. No one cared. I was left alone in my scrap world, and I enjoyed it there.

I liked my time in the junkyard because it allowed me to be free of all the bad things in my life. I could play with whatever I wanted, and the junk never judged me because I smelled or because my clothes were left-over from the 1950s. Aside from the cars, I also liked to light fires. In fact, I loved fire. I would make designs on the ground with gasoline and then light them up.

Sometimes I set fire to different pieces of junk just to see how they would burn.

I was only eleven then, but I was aware that I was supposed to be doing something different with my life. My mother's words still sounded in my head. Some days they rang stronger than others, but they were always there. I knew I couldn't let her down. I absolutely had to finish school, graduate from college, and get away from this family. But I was stranded here among the piled scrap cars. I was outside the rest of the world and free, and a large part of me didn't ever want to leave. There was no death here. For the time I spent in the yard, I was alone and content. Why would I want to change that?

So it wasn't me who initiated my return to school from junkyard life. The truancy officers really did exist in the 70s in New York. They showed up at our house one day to threaten my grandparents. I hadn't been to school in over a month, and they were not happy. But it wasn't so much their threat to remove me from custody that got me back to school. My enterprising grandfather knew that if they lost me, they would also lose the monthly check they received from Social Services for taking care of me. They collected welfare money for providing food and shelter for us children, but one of the stipulations in their contract with the state was that we had to go to school. No school, no money—that's how it worked. When the truancy officer made this perfectly clear to them, they sent me back to school fairly regularly, and my days in the junkyard were over.

And though my days in the junkyard were over, my days in the schoolyard had only just begun. It was in the schoolyard that I began to understand why my mother told me to get away from my family. She had to have known that not only was the family degenerate but her brother, my uncle, was a drug dealer. He took me under his wing on the schoolyard and had me selling pot to other kids.

Any family member who would have a child sell drugs at school to make money is not a family member worth having. Worse yet, my uncle's behavior was not only known by the rest of the family but also tacitly endorsed. My mother's words were like a backdrop to my life that gave me an intuitive understanding of right and wrong. And my daily life and experiences simply reinforced what she taught me.

Eleven-year-olds can't really change their families. They are stuck with the ones they are given. That was me. I had recognized that everything was wrong, but there was nothing I could do about it. I was a hostage of my own family. In those days, social workers didn't delve too deeply into the family life of the children they were supposed to protect. But in the end, it wouldn't matter what a social worker in Moriches, New York, thought because before too long we moved upstate, and I had the opportunity to actually live out my mother's last wishes.

Chapter 3

When I was twelve we moved upstate near the Canadian border to a town called Constable, New York. It was a little place that my uncle Ed owned. He was the same uncle who had me selling pot in Moriches. We moved because my grandparents had lost the junk-yard house down on the Island. Apparently Ed used to pay the rent there, and when he decided to move up-state he also stopped paying for their little house and scrapyard. When this happened my grandparents had no choice but to move all of us to Uncle Ed's farm.

Ed was the meanest man I've ever known. He was a disabled Army vet. He used to beat us bloody for just looking at him, and he seemed to get satisfaction out of hurting children. He hadn't been around all that much in Moriches, but now we had to see him almost daily. I learned pretty quickly not to make eye contact with him under any circumstance.

My brother Daniel couldn't stand to be near Ed at all. One day when I was in the hayfield working to clean the machines, Daniel must have talked back or said something that Ed didn't like. Ed beat him like he was a grown man. I remember the sickly sound his punches made against Daniel's face. Daniel was lying in the grass spitting blood up into the air. He was truly injured. Ed had done something to his ribs.

I ran and called police, and they showed up with an ambulance. When they arrived, Daniel didn't want to let them near him, not even to help him. He just kept saying, "I'll never come back here. I'll never come back here." I had to carry him to the back of the ambulance. I remember he waved good-bye to me as the ambulance pulled away. Nothing ever happened to Ed for doing that to Daniel.

Now I was going to live alone in a trailer on Ed's land. We all were going to live in several trailers and a few outbuildings that were scattered over the property. The specifics of our living arrangements are still a bit hazy to me. At times all of my brothers and sisters were kept together in the same place. But I think most of the time we were separated. I've talked to my younger brother Mike about this and my sister also, but we all have such different memories that it's hard to piece it together. Everyone was at different ages and saw different things. It's probably best forgotten anyway.

The one thing I'm sure of was that for long stretches of time they had me living alone in this rickety old trailer—but to call it a trailer might give the impression that it was habitable. If you've ever driven around the backwoods and seen an old abandoned trailer, rotted out and surrounded by a thicket of overgrowth, then you can picture my new place. The trailer had no water, electricity, or sewer. In the winter I froze; in the summer I scorched. The weather wasn't just bad for me; it was also bad for the chickens that were kept in one of the other rooms. This was what our move to upstate was like. I'd come from a rattrap to a chicken coop.

I can still recall the long car ride up and the hopes I had for our new and wonderful environment. My grandparents had told me I was going to a farm where there were meadows of flowers and chickens that you could hold. I watched out the car window as the city first came into view and then disappeared. As we drove north on 87, the cityscape turned into the suburbs of Westchester. When we crossed the Tappan Zee Bridge, the countryside became less and less populated until finally we passed the Catskill Mountains. On Long Island, I had never seen the mountains before, and so I was happy to have the view. Beyond the mountains we came to endless fields of green that continued for as far as I could see. As we passed countless farms, I imagined my future running through grassy fields—cows, chickens, maybe even a horse. Which farm was ours?

I had plenty of time to let my mind run wild. The drive from Moriches, New York to the town of Constable is something like 450 miles. When we finally got to the little town and pulled up the washed-out gravel road, my expectations piqued until I saw what they were calling a farm.

I had no idea at first why we were pulling up to the small trailer at the end of a washed-out gravel road. Maybe we needed to stop and pick something up from the poor neighbors before we headed on over to our farm. But as my grandparents got out of the car and my brothers and sisters followed, I realized that this once white, rusted trailer was the "farm" they had been talking about.

My uncle was waiting outside when we got there. He greeted us at the door by turning his back on us and walking away. I was afraid to even go inside the thing. In Moriches I at least had a home; now I was moving from a house into a tin can that properly belonged in my grandfather's long-gone scrap pile. On some nights I would have the company of one of my brothers or sisters. Sometimes I'd even be lucky enough to spend time with the rest of the family in their shack, or in some other trailer, but typically I was alone with all the noises of the forest outside and the bugs and the chickens inside.

And so began one of the more painful chapters of my early history. I had only two pairs of jeans that I wore on a rotation. I looked poor and I was poor. My shoes had holes in them, which I covered with duct tape, and the shirts I wore were always dirty. I smelled. Kids picked on me and harassed me all the time. Children can represent all the worst parts of human nature, and when they see another child who's different, whose teeth are bad, and clothes dirty, they can be so cruel. They turn that child into a target and create a ring around him. I was that kid. There was no safe place for me, either at home or at school. I often dreamed of going back to the junkyard where I was safe and free and could act like a kid. They made fun of the stains on my shirt, and once they discovered that I had only one pair of shoes and two pairs of jeans they taunted me relentlessly. They even named my jeans. I don't remember what they called them then, but some kid would always announce which one I was wearing that day.

The name of my jeans wasn't as bad as the name they gave to me. They called me "sea mold," which was apparently how I smelled. But at twelve years old, I couldn't help it. Whenever I did want to have a bath or wash my clothes, all I had to do was go down by the river and wash myself on the rocks, a practice that in the winter was nearly impossible. On days when it was cold and I was itchy with a rash, I would think to myself, "Life sucks." Actually, this was what I thought to myself most of the time—and yet I always believed it would get better. Even then, I began to form the absolute belief that I would make my life better. This very same belief gave me courage twenty years later when I worked in another dung heap in corporate America.

In my move upstate, there was at least one thing that had changed for the better, and even though Ed was a miserable son-of-a-bitch he did at least allow me to go to school. I don't actually know that he cared what I did, but since he didn't have anything better for me to do, like strip metal from junk cars, he sent me along to the local school. I'm sure he was happy to have me out of his way, too.

My grandfather still wanted me to work for him as he attempted to bring his junk collection up from Long Island. It must have had some value; at least it represented his life's work, so he was reluctant to simply leave it behind. But to move two hundred or so junk cars plus numerous other piles of scrap nearly five hundred miles through two separate mountain ranges is a difficult task for anyone, especially if he's on welfare. Yet he wouldn't give up on his plan. I don't know why he didn't just sell the scrap on Long Island, but he didn't.

I can picture him now, pulling up to our trailer one Saturday morning. He was in his 1959 International with a twenty-three-foot flatbed overloaded with trash from our old place. He stepped out of the truck. I was on the lawn playing with a toad in the grass, and he looked at me and said:

"Unload it!"

I replied, "You should just take it to the dump."

He looked at me like he would kill me. Had I have said the same thing to Ed, he probably would have, but my grandfather was a little more reserved, and so he just repeated his command. "Unload it now!"

This time I listened to him and unloaded his garbage into piles around the yard. I'd grown strong for my age by this point, both from fighting with the other boys at school and from being forced to do things like empty scrap metal and car parts from flatbed trucks. But this wasn't the only activity that helped me get bigger. I also began helping out on a nearby farm.

It was the summertime, and a local farmer named Ivan had asked Ed if he could do a couple weeks of work mowing the hay and splitting the bails for him. Since Ed was disabled, he couldn't do the work and so he sent me instead. At first Ivan was skeptical about what a little boy could get done. It wasn't that he didn't like me, or even that he didn't like children. This was a man's job, and he told me so from the first day. I soon proved I was up to the work, and he had me doing all sorts of tasks around his farm. Any farmer who makes his living from the land always has work that needs do-ing and neither the time nor the money to do it.

When he saw that I could work like a man and that I was competent at the age of twelve, he started to like me. He had also started to respect me. He told me one day that I could make more money using a pen than using a shovel. It was a strange thing for him to say out of the blue like he did, but he wanted me to know how he felt.

After the initial two weeks of work were up, Ivan gave me a job for the whole summer. He paid me two dollars an hour, but I never saw a penny of it. I was ex-pected to give it right to my grandparents, with grati-tude. This is not an unheard-of practice. It was just less common in the twentieth century then it was, say, in the 1830s. I read in school that Abe Lincoln used to be rented out for work by his own father. For his trouble he collected no money, but Abe grew strong, and so did I. Had I have taken any of the money Ivan paid me and spent a dime of it, chances are pretty good that I would never have seen Ivan again.

Ivan knew this also. He recognized how my family treated me. He saw that I had no clothes, or only dirty ones to wear, and that I always smelled. He knew that I was hungry, too, and he used to bring food out to the field for lunch. I never admitted to Ivan that this was all I had to eat for the day, and for his part he pretended not to know it either. He acted as if it were routine to feed the field hand. He would make comments here and there about my situation, like about making money with a pen, but he couldn't really speak up and tell me what he thought of my family. He made it apparent; he just didn't articulate it. But the way that he felt and the type of man that he was would become more apparent as time went on. The lessons that he taught me would also remain with me for the rest of my life.

Chapter 4

I was still living in the trailer by myself when I turned fourteen. It was wintertime, and I still had the chickens as trailer mates. None of us had heat. It was cold that winter. The front door to the house didn't close right, and I had to hang a blanket in front of it to keep the wind from blowing in. At night, I wore my clothes to bed and layered up with as many blankets as I could get. I know that in cold-weather camping people say you're actually supposed to sleep naked, but try telling that to a fourteen-year-old boy who's trying not to freeze to death in a trailer in the north country.

About December, those chickens froze to death. That was how much my family cared about me. I was loved as much as the livestock was, and they let the livestock die. I was also kept around for similar reasons to the livestock. In other words, the chickens brought in income, in the form of eggs. I also brought in income. They couldn't eat me, but every month the state sent a check to them because they housed me. But that was all they did. Just like with the chickens, they did the absolute minimum necessary to maintain a life that provided for them, and they were neglectful even in that.

That winter when the chickens died, I thought I was going to die. I was just so cold. Every night I froze, wrapped up in wool army-surplus blankets from Korea. The inside of my windows had ice crystals covering them. I slept with a winter hat on. One night I had a fever. I think I had pneumonia. I was in bed shaking, and I could see my breath I was so cold, but I was hot at the same and sweating under my clothes, which made it worse. My body ached like I was going to die. Then I forced myself up and walked out. I had had enough, and I never planned on coming back. I even had the wherewithal to pack up all my belongings. There wasn't much, and as a matter of fact, everything I owned in the entire world fit into a brown paper bag. The bag wasn't even full. It also contained no pictures.

It was snowing outside, and when I got to the road I had no idea which direction to go. I was like a prisoner of war who escapes only to find he doesn't know where to go. The blanket was wrapped tight over my shoulders, and the snow was blowing hard. I thought about Ivan, and I headed in the direction of his farm in Westville, the town just north of ours. Regardless of the fact that the two towns shared a border, Westville wasn't right around the corner. In fact, Ivan's family farm was about four miles from my house on Route 122. Nevertheless, I walked in that direction.

Upstate, the winters are brutally cold and windy. I was holding that blanket up to my chin as I walked to protect myself from the snowflakes that kept getting under my clothes and onto my chest. They melted when they got there. I was shaking and confused. I belonged in bed being taken care of, but no one was there to take care of me, and so I was walking in the middle of the night in a snowstorm. As I kept walking, the wind picked up, and my body hurt with every gust. I wanted to lie down.

Eventually, I saw lights from a house above me on the hill. There were patches of green grass scraped raw by the wind, and other places that were entirely covered by snow. I know I heard dogs barking. And then I sat down in the middle of the road. My legs ached, and my chest hurt. I just wanted to rest there a while until my body felt better again. I don't know how long I would have remained there like that, maybe until someone on the way to work found me frozen to death in the morning. But I didn't have to wait for that moment. Pretty soon some headlights came down the road toward me. At first I thought streetlights had come on, but then I saw the red pickup truck headed my way.

Ivan stepped out of the cab and picked me up by my armpits. His wife, Pearl, had spotted someone sitting in the road when she let the dogs out. She told Ivan, and he came out to investigate. He had no idea that it was me. He walked me to the passenger side and placed me on the seat. I was talking to him, but later he told me that I wasn't making any sense.

"Oh my God," Pearl said when he walked me inside the house. "Get him in here." I don't remember much from that night, but I remember her saying that when she saw me.

Pearl undressed me and bathed me. Then she put me in a warm cot and kept me alive. For several days she nursed me back to health with chicken soup and kindness. No one had ever really been kind to me before, and I developed a bond with her that would never be broken.

I don't know what my grandparents did while Pearl was nursing me back to health; no one ever said. They didn't come to visit me or send a card. But when I got to feeling better again, Ivan came into the room to talk with me.

"What do you want to do with your life?" He was always direct.

"Mom said I should finish school, but things aren't looking good."

"Your mom?"

"Yeah."

"Well, you can stay here. We'd like that. There's a spare bunk in the barn. It's not nice, but it's warm and dry, and you can use the bathroom and shower in the house."

The house was small, and he already had two daughters living in their own rooms. Offering living space in a barn may seem cruel, but it was the nicest thing anyone has ever done for me. And, like he promised, it was warm and it was dry. He went on to explain that I could live with his wife and two daughters, but that I'd be expected to do chores, and milk and care for the cattle. There were over three hundred head of dairy cattle on the farm as well as some two hundred heifers, which made for a lot of work for a boy to do. But I didn't mind. In fact, I loved the work.

"And you've got to get good grades." Going to school was important to Ivan. He was a strict man who believed in hard work and education.

"That's what I want," I said, and he smiled. Before I even understood what happened, my whole life and future changed. I now had a stable and caring place to live. It was like a dream come true. Ivan was going to give me a home and get me away from my family, and in return all I had to do was work and get good grades. He was granting me my mother's last wish. I couldn't have been happier with the arrangement.

My grandfather was not as pleased. But Ivan called him and told him where I was and that I was going to stay and wasn't going back to them. At first my grandfather argued with him, but it simply came down to the fact that my grandfather didn't want to give up custody of me because he didn't want to lose the income through welfare. I didn't care at all about the income I generated, and fortunately neither did Ivan or Pearl. They didn't have a lot of money either, but they wanted to see me on my way, and they knew I wasn't going to go anywhere living with the family I had.

Some people do good things just because they are there to be done. Ivan and Pearl had no obligation to me in the world. They certainly had little to gain by having me around. While I did do chores and helped with the cattle, my work was hardly an income-generating activity for the family. It helped, don't get me wrong, but they took me in because they saw it as the right thing to do. Period. And because they did what they did, they saved my life.

They also warned my grandfather that if he did try to take me back, they would get the police involved. With that, he left me alone. From that point moving forward, my family disappeared from my life, and I just worked toward graduating from high school. I still saw my brothers and sisters from time to time and would help out with clothes whenever I could. It was rough to know they were still in a horrible situation that I had gotten out of, but there was little I could do to help them at that time. And I still had some rough moments. At school one day the guidance counselor told me I had a 95 percent chance of going to jail. I don't know if he knew where I was actually living, but he was certainly well informed about my biological family.

"Listen," he said, "you've got no father, your mother is dead, you're nobody."

In retrospect, I'm not sure if he said this to me as a motivation of some sort, but I have a very strong suspicion that the man was just a fool, and so I told him: "You know, you're pretty stupid." And then I stood and left his little office. From that point forward I was only more motivated to succeed. I wanted to prove that man wrong. I wanted to climb out of this horrible place. And I did.

Chapter 5

It was summer in the Hamptons. The year was 1986. I was building and servicing swimming pools with a local company, and I felt like I was beginning my adult life. Instead of being trapped by my birth and early upbringing, I was now a high school graduate with military training and a good job.

After Ivan and his wife took me in, I'd had little trouble making it to school everyday. I was dressed in clean clothes, and I had a bath every night whether I wanted one or not. School wasn't too difficult either, and I didn't need to fight so often because the other kids generally left me alone when I was clean. They had also learned that picking on me was a losing proposition, and so they backed off or just accepted me. It was good to be left alone and to almost feel like I belonged. I also felt this sense of belonging when I started working at the Long Island Federal Credit Union, but it would escape me again when I accepted my dream job at an international bank that saw itself outside the law.

After graduating from high school, the one thing I wanted was to be in the military. I believed the discipline and hard work would do me good. In January of 1981, I graduated from the Salmon River Central High School, and in February of that same year I signed up for the United States Army, as an infantryman. I wanted to be on the ground with the men, and soon I was off to Fort Benning, Georgia. Boot camp was tough, but I was tougher. I got excellent marks in everything I did, from how I shot and cleaned my rifle to physical fitness and CPR. But I didn't learn discipline from the military as I thought I would. Instead, I brought discipline with me to the military. I still needed to learn a lot of things, but discipline wasn't one of them. This was why I did so well. Going into boot camp, I was in better shape than a lot of the guys coming out. When we did push-ups, a lot of the other guys would try to stop or cheat on the proper form. I never had to do that. In fact, because I had so little physical trouble, the instructors went after me, just to push me to the breaking point. If I finished a run first, the platoon leaders had me carry the picnic tables on my back. I leaned pretty quickly to finish my task, just not always first or fastest.

There were other aspects of being in the army that came naturally to me as well. Because I had been working on cars since I was eleven and had been fixing equipment on the farm for years, I had a good understanding of how to use and break down whatever I encountered. I was a quick study with anything mechanical. I also found that I liked to pore over the manuals and memorize the technical jargon. Part of this was because I wanted to be the best at whatever was in front of me, but the other reason was that for so long I never knew the names of anything I took apart. I might have known what an alternator was and how to take it out, but I had no idea what any of the pieces inside it were called. Now I had access to the technical information that had been outside of my reach for so long. All I had to do was take it out of the book and remember it. It was an opportunity for me to learn how things worked on a granular level. And this went for every aspect of my service; if there was a book for it, I wanted to know the technicalities and be proficient.

Knowing and understanding the world allowed me to feel normal. I had always been on the outside in a family that was so embarrassed about itself it wouldn't even let me have friends, and I didn't even read a book from cover to cover until Ivan made me. Now I didn't have to guess at the meanings of things; I could ask, or I could find out myself. I was normal; I belonged. I was on the inside.

But the army was not the experience I was searching for. I learned many things and got shipped around the country to different bases, but my days were spent mostly in drudgery and I was bored. I was honorably discharged after fulfilling the time required of me.

I went back to visit Ivan and Pearl immediately after my service. Pearl was so happy to see me that she had tears in her eyes when she greeted me at the door. She knew I would be around, but I hadn't told her exactly when I was coming, and so when I turned up it was a surprise. "You got so big," she said. Ivan was happy also. And as hard an old man as he was, he hugged me.

Later that night we discussed what I wanted to do with myself. I could have gone anywhere in the world. I had money in my pocket and in the bank. But there was only one place in the entire world I wanted to go to, and that was Long Island. I harbored deep memories of Long Island, eastern Long Island in particular, as if it were the core of human civilization and the only place in the world anyone should be. While Ivan didn't share these sentiments, he agreed that I should go wherever I felt most comfortable, and he gave me his blessing to head out in my chosen direction.

Soon thereafter, I bought a used car, though not from my grandfather, and drove down to the Island. The drive was as I remembered it: long. After about seven hours, I reached Manhattan. It was another hour before I got out to Moriches. Even though I had such a rough time here, I still thought of this place as my home, and I wanted to see what it looked like after all this time.

The old house had been torn down and all the junk removed. When I saw the empty lot, I felt relieved. It was like a cancer was removed from my memory, and now I could go on having good feelings toward Moriches without its being marred by this eyesore. The only thing I wasn't happy about was that I didn't get to tear the place down myself. I had often dreamed of buying the house and building my own mansion on the property. But I could handle the fact that someone else got to demolish this scrap heap without me.

I was on Long Island only a few days before I arranged to work for a company that built and serviced pools in the Hamptons. (The Hamptons, by the way, begin just one town from Moriches.) I never had trouble finding work. I just looked in the paper and answered the advertisement. For the interview, I drove over to a house down on the bay where a crew was digging a pool. I pulled up and stepped onto the crushed gravel driveway. The house was two stories, with weathered cedar shakes for siding and some modern art in the front.

When he saw me pull up, a man stepped out from his backhoe and came over to me.

"You John?"

"I am," I said.

We talked for a few minutes as he sized me up. Then he said, "You worked a farm and did the army so you know how to get out of bed and show up for work?"

"I can do more than that."

"Well let's just start with that for now. You're hired." We shook hands, and that was that. I was now building pools for the wealthy Manhattan executives who summered on the east end of the Island.

I was happy to have been hired so quickly. I was used to life the hard way. When I'd wanted something normal, such as going to school like the other kids, I couldn't have it. I was just twenty-one, but still I had lived most of my life under the shadow of that family, and so I was used to the idea of my wishes turning sour. Walking onto this jobsite, the idea that the man would turn me away had been heavy on my mind.

The work was hard. We dug holes and poured the pool walls, or spent the time fixing the broken filters or torn lines. I learned how to build a pool, which is really not useful unless you plan to make a career of it. But what I really began to take note of was what the homeowners did to make a living. I recognized quickly that few people who owned houses in the Hamptons and had enough money to add a pool also worked with their hands. Instead they were doctors or lawyers or accountants, and that's what I wanted to be also. I was reminded of what Ivan told me back when I fourteen: "You can make more money with a pen than with a shovel," he had said. And I was seeing that maxim played out in the Hamptons in living color.

You may think it strange that I would only have this realization at twenty-one years old, but from what I had grown up in, it's no surprise that this was true. I had had almost no experience with anyone who had money. While I had a normal life when I moved in with Pearl and Ivan, we were still so removed from the world that it was difficult to get an accurate view of things. But on Long Island, the hub of civilization, and in the Hamptons specifically, I got the whole picture. I knew then that I didn't want to be working with my hands for much longer and that I had to go to college so I could have one of these houses and one of these pools. If all I had to do was work for it and keep my focus, then I could pull it off just fine.

Another driving factor in this decision was that I was dating a girl at the time. Her name was Christine, and she lived locally in East Hampton where her father was a self-employed accountant. I saw firsthand from him how you could make your own life if you tried. And while he worked hard and kept long hours, he was also his own boss. It wasn't like in the military or on the job-site where people issued commands that you followed to the letter. He made arrangements with people and then fulfilled his end of the contract, and they paid him. And while his clients were his bosses, they stood on an equal footing with one another.

His was the type of life and the sort of business relationship that I wanted, and I knew the only way to get it was to continue my education. At the same time I was admiring her father, Christine was signing up for fall classes at Suffolk County College in Selden, New York, not so far from Moriches. She encouraged me to enroll as well.

"You have to do this, too." She knew how much I wanted to succeed, and she understood my drive. I knew college was the way for me to do that, but at first I was reluctant. I'd had my share of successes, but I was harboring memories of a failed childhood that loomed over everything. I was combating a nagging sense of failure that was holding me back. That was until Christine's father gave me a little more motivation for going to college.

It's funny enough to remember now, but a few days after she had been prodding me to take classes, she came to me and confessed that when she'd told her father of the idea, he laughed.

"What's he going to do in college?" he said. To him I was just an upstate farm boy with infantry experience and a job building and cleaning pools in the Hamptons. What business did I have taking college classes? When she told me this little fact, I was furious, but just like when that brilliant guidance counselor upstate had told me that I would never amount to anything, his words only helped to add fuel to my fire. I hated the idea that anyone would laugh at my dreams or think my desires weren't real, and so not only did I sign up for classes that night, I decided to become an accountant like he was, and signed up for Accounting 1. I knew it would be hard work, but I was ready for the challenge.

Chapter 6

Bill and Tony owned a vacation house on the Great South Bay in Mastic Beach. They were an openly gay couple, even though in the mid 1980s it was typical for gay life partners to keep their lifestyle very private.

I met them while working on their backyard pool. They were pleasant clients to work for because they didn't look down their noses and over their sunglasses and martinis at the "laborers." They would even strike up conversations on some afternoons. It was in this way that we came to know and respect each other. I was at ease sharing stories about my past, and they were at ease with who they were in front of me. They were a couple of guys who had had their own struggles and understood what it was like to be on the outside of life. They asked me about my plans for college and my career goals. It was Tony who first hinted at the idea to help me and ran it past Bill. The idea was that, I would live rent free in the Mastic Beach house during the off season with the understanding that I would act as caretaker and also do a few improvements on the property.

Now this was an opportunity I couldn't deny. I had a place to live and steady income, and I also I had classes to take and a future to look forward to. As obstacles to my plans were moving out of my way, I felt I would really get through school and find my pen-holding, businessman career after all.

My life was beginning to unfold the way I wanted it to, but the pace was also picking up to an almost breakneck speed. I was living in Mastic Beach and driving just twelve miles north to the Seldon Campus of Suffolk Community. I enrolled in early morning classes in order to have the better part of the day open to work. Free rent or not, I still had to feed and clothe myself. Then there was gas and car insurance.

When the summer ended, the pool-building business in the Hamptons ended with it, and I had to go out and find another job. My acceptance letter to Suffolk came when I was looking for work. I was happy about it until the bill came. At that my stomach churned. I had no idea how I was going to pay for it all. I had some money in the bank from work, and money from the Army, but it was nowhere near enough to cover the cost of tuition and books. And the books were another thing altogether. I couldn't believe how much they charged even for used ones. The bookstore charged almost sixty dollars for the textbook for one class, and this was in the eighties when the dollar was worth something. It was also before Amazon or the Internet so you were pretty much stuck for options.

I began searching for another job as soon as I got the bill. I cruised around in the area right around campus and went into every gas station, office supply store, and restaurant I could find. Not one of them was hiring. It wasn't until I went into a 7-Eleven that I got a lead for a job in the Ronkonkoma store, a couple of towns west of campus. At first I was concerned that my commute would be so long. I wanted to save on time and gas money, and I didn't want to be driving all over if I could avoid it. But I couldn't avoid it. I drove to the 7–Eleven, and they hired me on the spot. The job was part-time, just twenty hours per week in the afternoons, so my scheduling with school worked perfectly. Ronkonkoma also wasn't the busiest 7-Eleven in the world, and I could often get away with some reading while I was sitting behind the counter waiting for the customers.

I was so happy to get the part-time job. However, twenty hours a week at minimum wage wasn't enough to buy books. Bill and Tony came through for me again. They had a lot of friends in the area, who, like themselves, were just summer people. They needed work done on their houses, too, and they hated to have their vacations interrupted. So on the weekends Tony would connect me with various homeowners. Some of them needed their toilets fixed or lights hung, holes patched or decks built. Whatever they needed done, I did, and if I didn't know how to do it, I learned. Hardware store guys and lumberyard guys sometimes know what they're talking about. You have to ask around a little before you find someone behind the counter who knows how to install the stuff they sell, but if you're persistent you'll get a guy who can tell you how the skylight should be installed, or how a door is hung. And this was how I made my living and paid my way through Suffolk.

I worked all the time. I was in school in the mornings. In the afternoons and at night I worked at the store and then studied. My weekends were always fully booked with small jobs here and there from Tony and Bill. The main thing I recall about this time above everything else is how tired I always felt. I never had enough sleep, and when I wanted to sleep in on the weekends I had to work on summer cottages. I was becoming both physically and mentally drained.

I had no time for anything. A few times when I took Christine out on dates I nodded off at the table. It's funny to think of now, but I was so tired I just kept closing my eyes to give them a rest.

"Are you sleeping?" she would ask me. "No, no, I'm awake," but when I closed my eyes again she got mad at me. I felt sorry, but there was nothing I could do. I was studying for a final, writing a paper, and working two jobs. I shouldn't have even asked her on a date in the first place. But I wanted to make her happy, and now I was falling asleep across from her at the dinner table—a diner which I could hardly afford, but I was determined to pay. It was tough. And school was getting difficult, not just because of the workload but because a lot of the other students weren't really serious about their education. There were so many of them who just wanted to get stoned and drunk and party all the time.

This is not a reflection on the school itself, but a reflection of the attitude of a lot of the students who were just out of high school. The difference where I was concerned was that I was paying for school on my own. I was serious, and I was careful about who I hung out with because of this. Back on the farm, Ivan always used to say, "You are who you hang out with." When he said this, I never really thought anything of it, but it stuck with me. Now that I was at school with people getting stoned in the parking lots or drinking right after classes, his words rang through my head: "You are who you hang out with."

I was ready to move on from Suffolk County College. It was only a two-year school offering associates degrees, and from the day I enrolled I knew it was just preparation for a better-known four-year school where I could get a BS or BA degree. The only thing I was focused on was perfecting my grades for the move. It was also at this time I noticed I had certain educational weaknesses. While I had graduated high school, my schooling had really only begun when I lived with Pearl and Ivan. And while I could pass a test and learn anything you put in front of me, I had a gap in my learning. I don't mean I was stupid. But you do actually learn something in all those years of middle school and high school if you pay attention or are made to pay attention. I knew the gap was there, and I was not only trying to get the highest grades possible at school but I was also soaking up everything I could learn. I had to reinforce my foundation. I saw everything as a learning experience, even the small cultural cues people unknowingly give off that they learned somewhere in those early years of schooling I missed. But I was catching on after all.

After my first semester I began to research other colleges. I soon focused on Dowling College in Oakdale, New York. I was in awe of the campus. I know this isn't the way to judge a college, but the school sits on a former Vanderbilt estate on the Connetquot River. The original mansion and several of the outbuildings were used for classes. It was beautiful and historic, and the buildings represented business, enterprise, and wealth. Dowling also offered the course and degree program I was studying. It was also known for its competitiveness and the success of its students. Again, Ivan's words came to mind: "You are who you hang out with." And I wanted to be around serious students.

I was ecstatic when I was accepted. The cost of tuition was nearly three times that of SCCC, but I knew I would find a way to pay for it. By now I had developed a ritual of work and school that I could handle. And with the twenty or so hours at 7-Eleven along with my construction and house-maintenance jobs, I could afford the cost difference. I wasn't happy that I would be spending myself down to the last penny. I was happier, though, to be in a position to succeed. Classes were much more difficult than at Suffolk. Professors were more demanding. Course materials were much deeper. I was required to devote even more time and effort and energy into my studies. If I was tired at Suffolk, I was exhausted at Dowling. I had time only for work, school, and sleep; nothing else, and this included Christine.

It was difficult, but I was learning, and I was bringing my grades up. I was aiming for the coveted 4.0, but that was a tough target to reach. Still, one of my professors told me I was a natural. It was interesting that accounting just came to me considering that I had never had any money to speak of in my life. But accounting wasn't just money; it also encompassed the rules, the process, and the numbers—these I could understand.

I viewed accounting just like any other machine or complex device. The first step I took was in understanding an overview of the whole—like how, in an automobile, I knew what part the alternator played before I knew all the individual parts of the alternator. And this was how I saw college and learning in general. You started with the introductory classes, which were just crash-course overviews of a whole subject. The scope and speed of the introductory classes also served as a way to cut out students who weren't really paying attention. Once you got through these, you got to move onto more specific topics with tighter focus. Again it worked in the same direction as with cars: first you saw the car, then the parts that made up the car, and then you learned what made up the parts themselves and the names they had.

I was interested in the whole grammar of accounting. Understanding the technical terminology gave me a great sense of accomplishment. I used to recite the terms and definitions to myself on the way to work and take flash cards with me behind the counter while serving up coffee. I was so tuned into this because it was the foundation of the big picture that I needed to understand clearly. The world of money, what money does, where it goes and how it gets there became my life.

Chapter 7

I graduated from Dowling College in 1990 with a bachelor's degree in accounting. My advisors suggested that I enroll in an MBA program. I was interested—college was great, and I wanted to continue my formal education—but not now. I had grown up *doing* all my life: from the farm to the Army to home improvements. Now I wanted to apply what I had learned and begin to build my career. For me, the day I graduated was the day I truly started *doing*.

It wasn't long after graduation that I picked up *Newsday* magazine and saw an advertisement for a job opening at Pan Am Federal Credit Union. I felt a shock. I had been looking all over for work and had calls in to as many people as I could, but to just stumble onto the job like I had was a stroke of good fortune. I remember having the feeling that this was going to be it. First I researched the credit union and found out as much about the people there as I could, and then I drafted what I thought was the perfect cover letter and sent it in with my resume.

I heard back from them in two weeks, which is still pretty quick in this industry. I had the interview on Tuesday morning. It was late May, early June, and beautiful. In the springtime Long Island can look like one big garden with highways for walkways. I had my suit pressed and laundered and felt confident as I drove to the credit union. I was forty minutes early because I didn't want to risk one of Long Island's famous traffic jams, not on the most important day of my life. I was, after all, a homeless farm boy with infantry training who was building pools and working at a 7-Eleven; I didn't really expect that bankers were going to give me the benefit of the doubt if I was late.

Even though I was confident and felt like this was meant to be, there was this other secret part of my mind that was telling me I would be a failure and that this was the day I'd find out. The longer I sat in the parking lot waiting, the louder the voice became. I had full conversations in my mind where I started to think that I must be kidding myself. Like I was just a fraud, and today I would go in and the man interviewing me would simply uncover me. He would strip off my suit jacket like a demotion and tell me to go pave roads for a living. And then he would mark my name down in a notepad that every other credit union and white-collar employer in the world would read. Next to my name it would now say: "laborer." And that would be that.

My interview was for ten a.m. I found my confidence and entered the office at a quarter to ten. I smiled at the secretary. She was an older woman, and she smiled back. But she cut off her smile faster than I would have liked, and I took that as a bad sign.

"So you just graduated from Dowling?" she said when I was done filling out the application.

"I did, yes ma'am." I knew I was through now. The way she pronounced *Dowling* made me think that this was a school they routinely rejected candidates from.

After waiting for a little while longer, I was escorted into the conference room to meet a man named Michael. Apparently he would be the one who took away my dream, but a strange thing happened as he stood to greet me. I knew that I belonged here. I was certain of it when he reached out and shook my hand.

"Nice to meet you, John, have a seat."

And so I sat, and he asked me questions while holding the copy of my resume I had sent.

"Upstate, huh? And you used to do farm work."

I hadn't even put half of my real life into my resume. I only included the parts that showed solid work experience, reliability, and education, and didn't leave any timing gaps. He couldn't see the misery, despair, and neglect. But I think my resume showed more than I intended it to. Or, at least, Michael could see more.

"You know, you're the type of candidate I like. We get a lot of people through the doors who have frankly never lifted a finger. Their college grades are fine, and they have some interning experience. But from what I gather from you and from your resume, I like your drive and your ethics. I could use both here."

Michael didn't hire me on the spot. There was a required second interview. But, as he said, "Unless something surfaces between now and then that disqualifies you, you've got the job."

He shook my hand. I walked through the doors and said good day to the secretary. But I had to keep from screaming as I walked into the parking lot. I had made it in. I had heard so many horror stories of people waiting months and months for a job offer. I couldn't have been happier with having my first interview be a hit. There was no doubt in my mind that I would take the position straight off when they offered it to me. I didn't need to search the market for the right opportunity. The right opportunity for me was the opportunity that first presented itself because I knew that all I needed was experience. Hard work and a little personal sacrifice hadn't bothered me so far, and they wouldn't bother me now. I would dedicate myself to whatever the credit union needed me to do. I would be always preparing myself for the first promotion.

Later that afternoon I called Pearl to tell her that I thought I had gotten a job at a credit union. She and Ivan were thrilled and proud of me. The only shadow on that lovely Long Island spring day was the pang of sadness at the fact that my mother wasn't there to tell. I didn't know her for very long, but I remembered her, and I remembered what she said to me. Her advice had come to shape my life. I really had accomplished what she wanted me to accomplish.

Chapter 8

A few weeks later, Michael called me personally to say that I had been hired. I would start the following Monday as an accounting clerk. But because it was a relatively small credit union, I had the responsibility of keeping almost all their financial records. The job was daunting at first. I had only a brief training period where they showed me the ins and outs of the software they ran, which was, of course, different from what I had learned in school. After that, I was instructed on various entries, policies, and procedures. And after that I was expected to produce. The reports came through me. Suddenly I had gone from a student to a cog in the machine, but a cog that had to be reliable. And this was the hardest part for me to get over at first. There was no room for error. The CFO's financial decisions depended on my bookkeeping.

I was proud and eager to succeed. I knew that if I could hold on beyond the first few months, I would find my groove. I was well aware that I just had to make it beyond the learning curve. I was literally in a position where I was expected to learn fast. One night I called a professor from Dowling with a list of terms I had never heard. He helped late into the night with some of the more convoluted accounting steps of a project I had been working on, like contra entries and various methods of depreciation and future values. This was really the only time I had to ask for outside help, but I couldn't have done without it. Pan Am expected me to know these things, and so I found a way to know them.

The pressure subsided after four or five months as I reached the top of the curve. Accounting has standard practices. When people begin to get creative is usually when some type of irregularity is involved. The consistent use of the proper standards sets those transactions apart. I settled in then, knowing and understanding the job. My books and records were in perfect proof. But I began to get itchy to move on just as I had in other jobs. It was time to do more, to learn more. From around the time I moved in with Pearl and Ivan, I had begun to set goals, work toward them, achieve them, and move along.

"Would you consider moving me to a different position at some point?" I asked Michael one bitterly cold fall morning.

"You're happy with what you're paid, aren't you?"

He thought my motivation was monetary, but the money wasn't all that moved me. They were paying me well. My salary was already far in advance of what I had made at any other position I'd ever held. If I stayed here at this salary level with raises and promotions over the years, I knew I could build a fine family life and have the things I'd always wanted for myself. But this wasn't my only motivation. I found I loved to be challenged, and when I wasn't being challenged, and especially when I wasn't learning, I was bored. Sure, if the money was phenomenal, my wanderlust might have been satiated, but in this case what I really wanted was to press on to bigger and more challenging responsibilities.

When Michael was noncommittal about the possibility of my moving to a different position, I knew immediately that I would have to begin looking for a better job somewhere else. If he wanted to keep me, all he had to do was give me a little more room to learn.

If he had wanted to, he could have allowed me to learn other positions in the company. But he didn't. On his part, he needed an accounting clerk, and he had hired a good one. The banking business, ultraconservative at the time, wasn't known for rushing employees up the ladder either. Banking was still a one-job-in-your-life-with-a-gold-watch-after-thirty-five-years kind of business.

I picked up *Newsday* and began looking for another job. This time my job search was less anxiety laced. Now I was comfortable enough where I was, and so I could afford to "wait for the best opportunity." I just had to keep my eyes open for it.

I didn't have long to wait. Within two months I had spotted an open position at Long Island Federal Credit Union, and I placed a phone call to reach out to them.

It's always best to know someone reliable in the company when you're going for a job if you can. They not only can give you inside information about the organization's culture; they can also get your resume to the top of the stack. Some people would rather go through the job process as impersonally as possible. On the other hand, I'd rather do the talking for myself than have any piece of paper do it for me. I like to ask the interviewer questions. This was still the beginning of my career, but I had no trouble whatsoever in one-on-one conversations. I may be nervous in the build up to the meeting, though I think that first interview experience was an exception, but once I'm in the room talking with someone I know exactly what to do and say. There's no problem there.

The telephone receptionist gave me the address and the name of the man who would review my file. I drove over on my lunch break and dropped my resume off in person. The HR representative wasn't in when I arrived, but I met a few people who worked in the office. A few days later I got a call back from Cheryl at the desk. We compared availability and agreed on a Tuesday meeting. Rather than interviewing first with HR, she said I'd meet with Lou, who managed this branch of the credit union. I didn't know whether or not I would get the job, but I knew I was lucky to meet with a branch manager first. Just talking with him would be a good experience, and if I impressed him and didn't get the job I might still get a new contact out of the whole meeting. I thought I could win either way. I was young, educated, very employable, and being considered for a managerial position.

Tuesday morning was cold. There was still snow on the ground from the storm we had over the weekend. The Island didn't get hit that hard, but up in Westchester the news said it was a disaster. We were lucky in the way of snow accumulation, but we did get the wind, and trees had been knocked down all over the place, especially along the highways.

I drove over to the office of the Long Island Federal Credit Union. I had taken a "personal day" off from Pan Am. I was hoping that Lou would hire me. Of course, you hardly ever go into an interview not looking for the job you're interviewing for, but I also knew that just talking with the manager would help groom me for my future career. This positive attitude helped shape my view of the day and allowed me to drop the stress, as instead of looking at the meeting like it held dire consequences, I saw it as just a talk between two colleagues.

This is what I told myself as I walked past Cheryl to go into Lou's open office door. Lou surprised me at first because he was old. Not "older" either, he was seventy, and yet he had a spry, athletic look to him and silvered hair that made him seem youthful while still carrying the wisdom of his age. He smiled as I entered and asked for me to take a seat.

"Please," he said holding out his hand.

And I sat at a chair facing his desk. Behind him was a large picture window that must have been in there since the building went up in the fifties. I could see condensation at the edges where the seals were gone. The window looked out onto a row of hedges and a small field onto a wooded lot. It was snowing.

Lou started right off. "You've never been a manager?" And since he was holding the resume that I'd dropped off the week prior, he knew the answer to his own question. Suddenly this whole job interview became a lot more real and more than just a chat between colleagues. He was in charge, and he was questioning me. I nodded in agreement to his rhetorical question.

"Why do I want a manager who's never been a manager?"

"Because I have excelled everywhere I've been, and I've worked my way up on my own."

"Yes, you have, but you've never been a manager."

And then I was calm because I knew I had an answer to this question he seemed to be hung up on: "I've managed people both in building pools and as a property manager while I was in college. I not only had to organize schedules but also people and materials. I had to understand the needs of my customers and keep them and my employees happy. I now have some banking experience and a formal education. I've gotten a firm view of the industry."

He smiled at me then like a movie dad who's about to teach his child a lesson, but he didn't act on what he was thinking and instead began asking more technical questions about the business and about my responsibilities at Pan Am. He nodded his head when I finished describing my day to days. And then he went into asking me about the military, but when I finished briefly describing that time in my life and what I thought I learned and hadn't learned there, he stopped. He was holding my resume between his fingers, and he suddenly looked more closely at it. I even thought he squinted a little. At first I thought he saw a mistake, but then he asked me, "Did that farmer you worked for also raise you?"

I thought this was too personal a question that I didn't have to answer. He was a wise man, and I am sure he had conducted many interviews. He obviously put the facts together and came to his own conclusions. It was also fairly obvious that he liked me. And despite the fact that he was a bit cantankerous, he seemed to have an easy way about him with me.

A few weeks later I heard back from Lou.

"Congratulations, you're hired."

Chapter 9

"I hired you, John, because you have a sound understanding of the business, and I think you're willing to work as hard as I am. Other than that, your lack of knowledge is a benefit because it means that no one's gotten in there and taught you all the wrong ways to do things. Which means I don't have to go in there and rewire you. You're as close to a blank slate as I can get, and if you listen to me, I'm going to teach you how this business really works."

This was how Lou began my first day at the Long Island Federal Credit Union. And really, if I'm honest, the training I got from Lou both began and ended my career. He wired me the way he thought a banker must be wired, with an absolute stress on integrity and honesty. However, that wasn't the way HSBC thought a banker should be wired.

Really every day with Lou was a training day. He clearly loved what he did. At seventy he would drive most people past the point of exhaustion and then keep going himself. He didn't like complaining: "And I don't like laziness; when we have something to finish, I expect it to be done. That's that."

And that's just how he was. The LIFCU had begun to involve itself in acquisitions as a secondary strategy for growth. Lou involved me in this part of the process. Financial records were reviewed twice or more. Documents were audited and verified. Every *t* that was crossed and *i* that was dotted had to be OK'd by both Lou and me. This process not only ensured accuracy but also dual control. I was seeing and verifying what he was seeing, and visa versa. He would also quiz me on transactions, balances, and line items, which was an exercise for both our benefits.

One thing about Lou that I came to know well was that he knew nearly everything there was to know about the business, and he intended for me to know it as well. In addition to the real life work experience, Lou insisted that I take some graduate courses. He would suggest both the class and the professor. Under Lou's direction I enrolled in Asset & Liability Management and Fraud Detection. He enjoyed engaging me in conversations about my classes, which included some not-so-subtle quizzes.

Lou would actually "plant" incorrect entries in the system (not so hard to do those days, as general ledger entries were made with a paper document) as a means to see how closely I was paying attention. He was a fanatic for accuracy. In fact, he took it as a point of pride that he was going to teach me banking and the credit union business. I was his project at first, then his protégé. He taught me and molded me as if I were to be his legacy. Lou's interest in me and my career brought me under his wing in the relatively small world of LIFCU.

In addition to holding the position of president at LIFCU, Lou was an adjunct Professor of Economics at a local college. He could recite the history of banks and credit unions on Long Island, and worldwide for that matter, down to a granular level of what institutions got sold when, and who was buying and why. He also held some pretty strong opinions about the mistakes that had been made in the banking and finance industries over the years, and where the greed of the era appeared to be taking us. He had some pretty hard opinions on some big names, and he wasn't scared to express them. He was our LIFCU oracle, and he knew it.

Lou was actually partially retired. He certainly didn't seem to need the income. He loved the industry and thrived on the activity. It was a great benefit to me that he wasn't ready to head to Boca Raton and hang with the other retirees at the local cafeteria's early bird dinner special. He preferred to stick around and share his years of experience, knowledge, and wisdom. What he said about my being a blank slate, "a tabula rasa," was so true. I learned and kept learning every day.

The Long Island Federal Credit Union was at the time growing through acquisition. We were actively researching to acquire other credit unions that were not performing to credit union standards. This strategy typically gave us fifteen hours of work to do in our ten-hour workday. There was no stagnation or boredom.

Every potential acquisition provided the opportunity to research the financial institution, including its members (borrowers and depositors.) I was most interested in the large corporate members.

Acquiring another credit union required understanding and auditing that institution's financial statements. We had to test the quality of their assets (loans to their members) and the regulatory compliance of their loan documentation. We got actively involved to know and understand how they brought in business. We had to decipher why their performance was weak and decide if we were the right institution to turn their performance around. Any institution acquired had to be a right fit for LIFCU.

The tedious periods of our research were broken when we'd find indications that someone was hiding something. We'd dig deeper to uncover errors—innocent or not so innocent. We occasionally unearthed some shady business underway. Lou would look at me and just shake his head. Fraudulent activity was involved and uncovered in several cases. The worst was uncovered at the Carle Place Federal Credit Union. Executives were getting away with blatant acts of fraud. The largest single amount discovered was 1.4 million dollars of the members' money being embezzled by the very people who were elected, entrusted with, and responsible for the safekeeping of their funds!

I never lost sight of or ceased to respect the fact that the money on deposit came from the members. A banker's fiduciary responsibility was also a fact that Lou hammered home time and time again. When you flipped through computer screens and printouts of monetary figures, you could easily imagine that you could simply dip in and help yourself. But you couldn't. The money was not yours. It belonged to the hundreds and thousands of other people who trusted you. Credit unions, unlike banks, are not for profit. They don't pay taxes, and they don't pay dividends to the owners or members. They can, therefore, enjoy a greater profit margin and give back more in service and lower loan rates with higher interest on deposits to the members. The executives were not supposed to be helping themselves to the profits. But their actions were not just morally wrong; they were also illegal.

Fraud was sometimes simple to trace once you understood the trail that money left in a business. I often wondered if the people knew they were going to get caught eventually. I developed a theory that some guys just had a death wish. I didn't know any other way to explain or understand their behavior. It was certain that they were going to get caught. Eventually someone was always going to come along and look at the books—someone like Lou or someone like me. I firmly believed this until I got to HSBC, where it seemed that a good part of the bank itself was designed to hide what the other half was doing. They were large enough to protect themselves from intruding eyes. They were both too big to fail and too big to get caught.

It wasn't that I wanted to be detective, judge, and jury. I had developed a passion for helping people, which included doing the right thing. It was as simple as that. That was the mission of the credit union. To a large extent, this was exactly how our credit union functioned, and I wanted to protect its integrity. The fact that I worked at a credit union and not a bank was also a factor in my view of what the organization did for the customers. The credit union did help customers with loans and with better rates of savings because we didn't have to meet shareholders' expectations at the expense of those same customers. We simply had to meet our customer's expectations, and they wanted us to protect their money. In reviewing and auditing, I wasn't looking to hurt anyone. My purpose was to prevent hurt in the first place.

To cause a charge of fraud or embezzlement to be brought against a credit union and its executives was serious. We had better be damned sure that the records bore proof without room for doubt, because someone was either going to get fined or go to jail. I saw it happen several times. I didn't take my role lightly.

The experience working on acquisitions and the requisite investigations made me an expert at discovering fraud and parsing fraud from what was not. I could also analyze the financials of credit unions and make recommendations whether we should acquire or pass. The process had to be quick. If we missed irregularities prior to acquisition, then those irregularities would soon become ours. After you've acquired a credit union and you discover irregularities due to criminal activity and you allow it to go unreported, you have become complicit in the crime.

Once fraud was suspected, then detected, we went into high gear. Time was of the essence, as was accuracy. Careers and livelihoods were on the line: ours and those of the implicated. It was urgent, sensitive, and complicated.

I remember meeting with executives from another local credit union in their boardroom. Their boardroom was typical of a bank boardroom: it had a gigantic mahogany table, comfortably overstuffed leather chairs, and a carafe of ice water sweating in a tray in the center of the table. There were oil paintings of the former board members lining the walls—all old men. (I always looked for Mr. Potter.) The chief lending officer that I was speaking with had a heavy Long Island accent and an arrogant attitude. I was asking him for details on some of their loans.

"And why does this company you approved this loan to have no tax returns? We have no proof of income or ability to repay."

That was the first and only question I had to ask. He and I both knew it. He began to stutter as he answered me. His forehead was shiny with sweat. He cursed. The rest of the "gentlemen" around the table stood up. If it had been back in the Old West, I think there would have been a shootout. Right then at that moment, he knew it was all over. He had been caught. Some of his colleagues attempted to calm him down while he spit and swore at everyone else in the room. Lou and I were on our feet as the flight-or-fight response came over us. We had unearthed the first layer of his fraud, and he knew it was really the beginning of the end for him. I had this crazy thought that the old guys on the wall were ashamed of him, too.

"I'll come over this table," he threatened, but he didn't do anything of the sort. It felt good to catch him because not only was he committing fraud, he was also trying to destroy another employee at the bank who had suspected what he was up to. A few months later they took him out of his home in handcuffs. He had embezzled a million dollars, and I caught him.

We turned his credit union around to profitability and actually helped the people he had been bilking. That was my favorite part of the job. It wasn't about finding crooks, though there was some satisfaction there. It was great to turn around a company that had been circling the drain and preparing for bankruptcy because of fraud and mismanagement. It was good to actually help the people who had become hostages of the crime.

Once we acquired a credit union, there was a great emphasis on public relations, especially if there had been fraudulent activity that had made the news. The members were naturally nervous about who'd be handling their money. Their fears were legitimate. We had legitimate fears, too, as we could easily lose these customers.

It then became part of my job to show our members why it was in their best interest to stay with us. We had to listen and understand and show empathy for their concerns. We had to explain to them the safe-guards we had put into place to protect their finds. We had to be trustworthy to earn their trust. It was in this role that I built up a following, a customer base or what's called a "book" in banking vernacular. (A few years later in my career, I came to use the term "client list," which was HSBC's snobby version.) There were several reasons why I was so good at retaining clients. I had run the investigation and managed the acquisition. Therefore, I knew everything about the bank, from what was wrong with it before to where it was going and why it was going to succeed. I knew these things because I had planned and executed them. It was now my credit union, and I could defend it better than anyone. But sales weren't so difficult for me. I liked people and I liked to hear their stories, and they liked to have someone listen. I found out what they wanted and needed. Mainly, I cared. It is just who I am.

A professor at Dowling College had given me some career advice. He told me that while I might want to get right into a large corporation, I should also consider a small bank. He felt that I would get more hands-on experience that way. Big corporations can have a tendency to typecast, and employees can end up trapped doing one very specific thing (like pretending not to see fraud). You may very well excel at this specific thing (at HSBC, many would), but you'll struggle to learn anything else or get the opportunity to learn new positions. At a smaller institution you will be called on to do a variety of tasks using a variety of skills. The compensation at the smaller bank may be less, but the overall experience is greater for the future. I benefited by following his suggestion.

It might be strange to hear a banker say that he worked for more than money. But to begin with, I worked at a local credit union, rather than a bank, and saw my clients firsthand. Many clients I knew personally. I also knew how important each company was to our business. When you deal with hundreds of business clients rather than thousands, each one is integral to your own operation, and you treat them accordingly. In addition, anyone who works with money as digits has to know the real value of those digits. Put another way, if you only care about the numbers and what the numbers mean to you, then you have no concept of the impact these numbers can have out in real time. If you see money as just a number unattached to human activity, and if you don't make the connection between your own behavior and the value that money has, then you are liable to do anything.

This is a good place to make a point. The people who handle credit, debt, and money—not money in paper form but the numerical denominations that runs like blood through veins—if those people are not upright, law-abiding, and moral with a view of money's social function, then you have a casino, not a bank. I know what I'm talking about. When the stewards of money shirk or eschew their responsibilities to their customers, it's only a matter of time before their bank is distressed and under investigation. I used to conduct the investigations and make a play on their remaining assets, and so when I was on the side of operating our credit union I was very careful about how I behaved. And yet what I say about a bank becoming distressed when it gets outside the law is true, of course, only if that bank is not so large that it's above the law, or at least above prosecution, as it is willing and able to pay the fines the US Justice Department levies against it to keep it out of court.

I learned this lesson many years later when I pointed out to two of the internal auditors at HSBC that the amount of fraud I had found might result in a material loss for the bank. I had seen people go to jail for much less than what I was finding. But when I said this, they laughed at me.

"John, we've got two billion set aside to handle this stuff."

That was really all they had to say. I knew what they meant. When the number was small and local, people would go to jail, but when the number was big and national, even international, jail sentences were paid off, and criminals went free.

Chapter 10

After several years of working under Lou, I considered myself a professional banker. The process of identifying credit unions ripe for acquisition was routine. I looked for those with strong assets and declining revenues. I could also readily detect fraudulent activity and get to its roots. The books always told the tale of when, why, and where their money was moving. And while I might not know who exactly was moving the funds from the outside, it was always linked to someone inside.

Work was my life. I was successful, but I had no one to share it with. What is money if you have no family to share it with after all? But shortly after getting hired at Pan Am I was lucky enough to meet the woman I would soon marry and build a family with.

Janice and I were married in 1992. A few years later we had our first daughter, Sarah, in 1995. In 1998 we were blessed again with another beautiful girl, Cassandra. To me there was nothing more wonderful than having my own family. And after the way I had been raised as a child, my family made me feel like I had truly succeeded. Not only had I built a career at an institution where I was integral to the day-to-day activities—a place where I was making more money than I had ever imagined—but I was also the proud father of two wonderful daughters and husband to a beautiful wife. My family never had to go without. They would never need love or attention or material things. They had me to provide.

When I was little, I always knew that a better life existed, but I just couldn't see it from where I was. I always believed that I would have the better life that I wanted, but now it was here and I couldn't have been happier. From time to time, memories of how life used to be would flash across my mind and literally floor me. I would look at my own precious children and wonder how anyone could be so evil to a child. I treat my dog better than I was treated when I was little. He gets fed better, too. My mother was right about everything she told me. Getting away from that family was the best thing I ever did.

I was enjoying my work life at the credit union, too. Business was good. My client list grew, and clients referred friends, family, and business associates to me. The stock market's "dot bomb" era sent investors running back to the banks for safety. The real estate market was hot. The credit union's savings balances grew, as did their residential real estate loans.

But the little happy bubble we lived in was soon to be disturbed by ripples of the outside world. In 2008 the world began to experience a recession that was kicked off by a sharp drop in the markets. The recession officially started in the fourth quarter of 2007, measured and defined by three quarters of declining gross domestic product. By that definition we don't know we're *officially* in a recession until we've been there for nine months. But in 2008, the world began to wake up to what was happening. The Dow Jones Industrial average for the week starting October 6 saw its greatest ever drop of 18 percent in one week of trading. The recession was the effect; the cause was our country's out-of-control investing and lending activities from about the start of the new century forward. As early as 2006, there were clear indications of overvaluation in the housing sector. There were predictions that the housing bubble would burst. The year 2006 was really when we began to see values decline.

In late 2007 I received a phone message from Fran Rogers Personnel, an employment agency that specialized in finding talented individuals in accounting, banking, and MIS. They left a number of messages with me until my curiosity made me return their calls. I spoke with Bill Savage, a banking executive placement specialist (aka "headhunter"), and decided to hear him out because the economy was so uncertain. I was attempting to safely position my career in anticipation of the inevitable, as I was sure times of rough sailing were on the horizon. I thought that I should at least test the waters beyond the credit union.

"This is an opportunity for you to work at one of the most competitive international banks in the world." Bill's job was to sell me on HSBC, and that's exactly what he did. This is not to say he lied to me. I mean, how was he to know what was really going on at that bank? I remember at first how much I disliked the sound of his voice, but as he persisted, I got over that prejudice and tried to hear him out.

"HSBC is an employer of choice, hands down. They hire only the best of the best."

For everything he was telling me, I was still comfortable working on a smaller scale in a smaller institution. I had always wanted to rise as high and as fast as I could, but I had grown accustomed to the genuine community feel of our credit union. I raised this point with Bill over the phone. "I've grown partial to working on the local level inside a company that really is part of the community."

I'll never forget his answer for as long as I live, because I believed him. He said: "And that's exactly why HSBC is an employer of choice. It's not just a slogan when HSBC says they are the 'world's local bank.' That's how they do business."

This was the first time I had ever heard their slogan. I was impressed, but it would come to haunt me in later years as terribly ironic. Bill went on to explain to me why it was true: "And what it means for them is that you will really be operating within your local community on a level with how you're operating right now. In fact, that's how you'll be judged, by the book you build up in your branch market area. I mean, right now you have an impressive client list, you've participated in buyouts, and you've undone the books of some places. This is exactly what they need on the ground.

No matter how big or worldwide a company is, they need local talent that knows how the banking system works. They especially need efficient bankers who understand compliance and regulation and know how to spot waste and fraud. Without strong bankers like that operating at the local and even regional level, the company would never survive."

I started to talk, but he cut me off. "Just think about it. Honestly, you've built your career up until this point, and now you're being rewarded. The compensation package they're offering you is really second to none, with pension, 401K, health, and vacation, not to mention a generous incentive plan. Just think about it."

From that moment forward, I primarily thought of HSBC during my workday. I did some research into the company, but in retrospect I did the investigation through rose-colored lenses, or in this case, through green-shaded ones. I believed the bank was better protected from an economic downturn than my credit union. I also wanted what Bill said to be true about HSBC because I was seduced by the figures he had thrown at me and by the idea of moving into a global bank where my room for growth was nearly infinite. Comparatively, a move up the regional level could be slowed by downturn, and I could only go so far.

I had never been driven by greed or ambition alone. I saw this as a simple career decision. Going to HSBC would not only offer me the best compensation package, while still allowing me to operate at the local level; it would also allow me the greatest room for growth. I really liked the idea. It seemed to be the right choice.

Any piece of information I did find that spoke nega-tively about the bank I merely passed aside as the rav-ings of disgruntled former employees. Any bad news that surfaced was out of Europe or Asia; I shouldn't have to worry about that.

Before long I was more than just mulling over the prospects of joining the HSBC community. I had spo-ken with my wife about it, and she also thought it was probably the best course of action to take. I had also begun to feel increasingly uneasy as the markets con-tinued to weaken. Around this time a web site was put up called *Mortgage Implode*. Every day it listed banks that went under due to the residential mortgage loan crisis. At first they were small investment banks outside of our area that dealt only in mortgage lending. They didn't hold their own paper but instead sold it off to Wall Street. They made their money on the loan fees and points. They had been as aggressive in their lend-ing as the brokers on Wall Street were in packaging the mortgages and selling them to once-hungry investors. And the investors were losing their appetites as fore-closure rates rose. For the mortgagors, the "come on" initial low rate periods of their loans were ending. They couldn't afford their payments on the reset rate.

I didn't need to be a prophet to see the writing on the wall as the defaults began to grow in the Long Island market. There were also many people actually betting against the US housing market a year earlier in 2006. Historically markets never rise ad infinitum; they always fall sooner or later. It's a normal cycle. And I was confident that being inside one of the world's leading banks with a secure position would be the best insulation from any downturn that might come. My sentiment might also have come with age. As you get older and wiser, speaking generally, you want less risk in your life. I didn't want to have to worry about my children's college fund or my retirement. At the credit union, I knew of a lot of guys who had stellar careers, and who had better upbringings and better and longer educations than I, but had taken one too many risks. Worse, some had been pushed out on their own by market conditions and lost everything. There was no way I was going back to working at 7-Eleven when I was fifty so that we could live in an apartment in Queens.

Fear should never be a driver in your decision making, but you should certainly consider it. Couple the idea of economic insulation and security with the fulfillment of my ambitions to continue succeeding and accelerating up the ladder to levels I could never have imagined, on top of the idea that I could still remain local while working at the "world's local" bank, and I was in with both feet.

But anything that sounds too good to be true probably is, and yet, I could never have known what I would encounter at this bank. I thought maybe bad management might put me off, or that the job would relegate me to a desk, or that it would at worst become drudgery. All of these things I could handle, but I never imagined how entrenched the culture of corruption would be, or how far regular employees would go to protect themselves by protecting the company they worked for. Coming from where I was coming from, it was difficult to believe that perfectly innocent and right-meaning people would cover up for crimes they had no part in, but it makes sense when you consider they were just protecting their own jobs. And once a culture of corruption has been established, it's easier for everyone there to just go along with it.

All these consideration were for me to ponder after my termination from HSBC for poor job performance and tape-recording coworkers, just two years after taking the position. For now, I had made up my mind to join HSBC as a vice president, senior business relationship manager. My office would be in the Carle Place branch in Nassau County. After my meetings with Bill, I had to go through a litany of phone interviews with various company personnel. What's interesting is how the level of difficulty and intensity of the phone interviews increased with each new one. I think there were four interviews in all, starting with an interview with a very pleasant Long Island woman who opened by asking me very basic questions about my life and career. She didn't delve too deep into my childhood; I think she had the proper impression and was tactful enough not to want to press me on just how dysfunctional we really were.

I remember coming away with the distinct impression that HSBC was really a local bank. It may sound funny now, but the bank went a long way to prove that statement; and as I became more involved, I learned that although they functioned like a regular bank in many respects, what set HSBC apart was the lengths they forced their employees to go to make personal local connections with their customers. HSBC sought wherever possible to "out local" the local banks when it came to personal touch and regional knowledge and care. They couldn't make money any other way. If you banked with HSBC and thought they were just global automatons without local connections, then you would move to a local credit union or bank in a heartbeat, so they had to appear to care and to really be local.

This is a matter of smart marketing, and while they do try to force employees to care and to be local, they are not actually local. My other interviews bore this out. The accent on the other end of the phone was British, and the woman was certainly given the task of taking runs at me. The interview reminded me of the old good-cop-bad-cop routine, and this Englishwoman, although she could have been Indian or South African, had the task of playing bad cop. She did such a good job of it that I believed she was really that way in her day-to-day life. But I had no trouble with her at all. And once I realized she was trying to draw reactions from me, I went into action.

I just acted as I would when I was in the process of taking over another credit union sitting across from someone that I knew was either incompetent or had been committing fraud. In those situations, no matter how tense or impassioned the conversation got, I would just stick to the facts. Keeping logic and emotion in their proper place was effective in keeping the conversation on track. If you allowed your emotions to get the best of you and said the things you felt, then you'd go down a road you or the other party had no business traveling down. It's like when football coaches give their players scripts to use when speaking to the press so they don't make mistakes. "The other team played hard today; we were happy to get a win." "We have to take this one game at a time." "Every game is important." "My teammates are the reason we won." "Our coaches did a great job."

I basically stuck to this strategy when I sensed her trying to get a rise out of me. But once she realized I had taken this tack, she tried to change my course. She wanted me to come out of my shell, and started to badger me: "But wouldn't you want to say more than just that? You don't want me to come away from this with only basic information, do you?" But really that was what I wanted her to come away with. I am still not exactly sure what she was after. I had never had an interview that was so confrontational before. Interviews were always impersonal, and sometimes irritating; they were never directly personal and purposefully irritating.

After forty-five minutes it was all over. There were just a few more interview levels after that. All these interviews were conducted by industry experts who just wanted to gauge my understanding of the business and the local area. In these conversations I excelled. At the end of one interview, the man who conducted it actually congratulated me on my knowledge and my answers. I've never had this happen before. And since I've helped out with the job interview process on the hiring side, I know that you don't want to give the candidate too much encouragement no matter how well you personally believe he or she did, because in the end the decision is not just yours to make and the candidate still may not get the job.

When this process concluded, they made me wait a few weeks and then informed me that I had gotten the position. The job would start in January of '08. I would have several weeks to conclude my business here at the credit union and to tender my resignation. I did feel some trepidation in leaving. I had given many years to this company and felt an attachment to my coworkers and colleagues. I felt some pangs of guilt that I was abandoning a ship that would flounder without me. But then, I might have been giving myself too high an estimation. They would be all right. I wasn't betraying anyone. I was simply moving on to a better opportunity. Lou understood this right away. He congratulated me wholeheartedly and wished me the very best.

In spite of well wishes, leaving was bittersweet. Everyone and everything in both my professional and personal life told me that I had made the right decision, and yet I still felt a pang of regret moving on. But as with many changes in life, once you've made the decision, any delayed trepidation just worsens the process of change. While I was still at the credit union, I felt that I was joining another world, and the former world of my early career was over. It was as if before my eyes the people and places I had known for so long and grown accustomed to were disappearing into the background, a memory, but a good one this time.

Chapter 11

I regretted leaving, and I didn't regret leaving. I felt a sense of loss in the same way you do when you graduate from college and move on successfully to the next stage of life. Even if I knew what was to come, I don't know how else I could have behaved. It was more than just chasing after money; moving to HSBC was taking the next step. I had been inducted. They had actively recruited me, how could I turn away such an opportunity?

To ask this question is to show regret, as if an error were made that cannot be turned back on. And to an extent this is true, but I could have stayed back on the farm after all, and I didn't do that either. This was the big leagues, and I was here to play, and so I switched offices with a sense of excitement about the future I would build, with just a bit of melancholy.

A difference I noticed immediately at HSBC was the revenue focus within the bank. Credit unions have the fiduciary responsibility to protect their client's money, while banks are profit driven and have to answer to their shareholders. I knew that I was in a different world and working under a different philosophy. But it wasn't as bad as I make it sound. It is true that banks are absolutely driven by profit, and yet I still had the sense of helping people. As the business relationship manager for the Carle Place Branch of HSBC, I had to seek out and acquire new accounts in Nassau County and keep and maintain the existing portfolio of business clients. I loved this aspect of the job because it brought me close to the people I was serving.

I remember that in my first week I was referred to an attorney who operated out of Carle Place, just a few streets away. I knew he handled financial interests in Manhattan. I placed the call cold, got his secretary on the phone, and asked for him by first name. I've made enough cold calls to know that if you fumble the introduction with a secretary, he or she knows right off the bat that you're selling something. But if you strike the right note of authority, familiarity, and kindness, then you can often sail right through the door as though you're a trusted friend. It's just a matter of how they perceive you. Some assistants and secretaries won't give anyone the time of day. Salespeople generally do not understand that what the administrative assistant or secretary thinks of you carries a lot of weight with his or her boss.

On this day, I struck the right note and was put through to Henry Glennfeld. He wanted instantly to cut me off, but he was polite, and before he could say good-bye, I asked him when the last time the relationship manager contacted him from his bank.

"Has a manager at your bank ever called you before? Do you have a business relationship manager?" When he didn't answer, I knew he was going to listen to me. "At HSBC, the world's local bank, we collaborate with each of our clients personally to help them achieve their business and personal financial goals. As your business relationship manager, I can promise to you that we are second to none. We are a global bank, established in 1865. Our clients' needs are supported by vast resources to enable us to provide the highest level of service. Because of this position we can readily withstand local cycles of economic uncertainty." My pauses between sentences allowed him time to "uh uh" and "mmm" in understanding with a bit more enthusiasm and interest with each pause. I was encouraged. "HSBC is local; HSBC is international. When other large banks want to move money over borders, they use HSBC." Now I heard, "Tell me more" from Henry. I continued, "We employ a disciplined approach to mutual communication with our clients that ensures that the issues most important to you are thoroughly addressed! Please keep me in mind; you have my number, and I do answer my phone."

Within a week he had switched his accounts over to HSBC. Apparently his last bank had irritated him one too many times, and I called him at just the right moment with the right opportunity. Sales work that way sometimes. People can develop a fear of calling prospects. Some people are just afraid to fail, or maybe they don't believe in the product they're selling. Either way, I had no problem with cold calls. I thought of prospects as clients I didn't know yet. I also had no reservations about the product I was selling. My job was to develop and maintain relationships with business customers. And I knew banking. In fifteen years of acquiring and retaining not only new clients but also whole institutions, I knew the industry like the back of my hand. I knew it so well I would dream about the flow of money through the bank, and of protecting clients. I saw money like blood, and I saw banks and credit unions as veins. I knew when something was wrong with the blood, and I knew when something was wrong with its circulation. So when I talked to a client, I came from the position of a physician with years of practice in a very specialized area of the human body. And when that guy talks, people understand that he knows.

I had complete faith in my product because of the amount of time and energy HSBC from a corporate level put into developing client relationships and customer service. Banking is a service industry that often believes otherwise. The first cardinal rule of banking is to protect the money; the second is to create relationships with clients. That is the foundation. If you can't protect clients' money first and foremost and you can't make them happy or don't have a relationship with them at all, then there is no point to your services. Just because you're a large bank, you may get some traffic because people know no better than to bank with you. But not everyone is so out of tune. Customers can tell you what they think of you with their feet; there is plenty of competition for their business. Bankers don't know they have lost a customer until he or she is long gone. Our communication plan with our clients at HSBC was well structured. In addition to knowing what our clients needed, we knew if they were unhappy and had the opportunity to correct any issues before the client walked. We were "dedicated to providing an unmatched level of service."

I was growing loyal to HSBC, and I was happy that my love of dealing with the clients and making relationships was as appreciated here as it had been at the Long Island Federal Credit Union. There may have been more emphasis on the revenue at HSBC, but at first, anyway, I was doing exactly what I loved. I was creating new relationships, and I was helping out old clients. I had brought a lot of business over with me from the LIFCU. Many of these people didn't leave the credit union entirely at first, but they opened new accounts with me and used me to exploit the opportunities that such a large and powerful bank offered them.

My work life at the Carle Place Branch was great. The one exception, and it was a problem that everyone in the bank shared, was that the computer systems were terrible. And I say systems because there were multiple computer programs from location to location doing the same things in an overlapping, convoluted network of inefficiency. They still worked in DOS, and this was 2008. The old timers used the DOS program because they still had access to it, and it was more efficient than the newer Windows operating system. There were probably seven separate programs that I had to learn at HSBC, none of them integrated, and a couple of them were there just to enter information that should have been captured on one or more of the other programs. As I'm writing this now, I'm just reading an article that HSBC's new CEO has announced that one of his plans for making the North American banks more efficient is to streamline the computer systems. Better late than never!

HSBC customers were at the mercy of the computer system, too. Good luck to them in getting current balance information! The computer system was not real time, so balance information was "as of yesterday's close of business." This crazy maze of computer programs at HSBC actually aided in the fraud. As errors were inevitable and routine because of the confusion, opportunity presented itself for those who chose to take advantage of the complexity. This design flaw was not a part of any scheme to launder money; it was simply a side effect of running a massive corporation where it becomes so difficult to change systems that it was just as easy to simply add layers.

I was stunned one day to see that the tellers typed up cashier's checks—yes, typed on a typewriter. You may imagine the use of typewriters or the old slide credit card imprinter still being in use at the small credit union. Not so. They had up-to-date, user-friendly, and streamlined computer systems. At the credit union, the head of IT knew what we required in a customer information system and to remain in compliance to regulations. He was not just the IT guy; he was also a banker. He made sure we had the system we needed.

As to the unnecessary complexity that the HSBC system presented, I've come to learn over time that whenever you're dealing with either an individual or a company, wherever there is unnecessary complexity there is usually fraud or lying. It's much more difficult to lie out in the open in black and white, but when the open field is a tangled thicket and black and white is a million shades of gray, it's hard to spot a lie for the truth and a truth for the lie. "Like separating pepper from fly shit," which is an expression I first heard on the farm.

The computer system shortcomings aside (and this was a big problem to "put aside"), the branch manager, James Duggan, was one of the best bankers I have ever had the pleasure to work with. When I was hired, I was told that I reported to our segment leader, who supervised all of the business relationship managers on Long Island. We would also report "on a dotted line" to the branch manager. The senior business relationship managers, or SBRMs, had varying impressions of what the dotted line meant, and as a result, most of the SBRMs had a contentious working relationship with their branch managers.

James and I worked together collaboratively. He was experienced, intelligent, and approachable. He treated our "team" with respect. He shared his experiences rather than lectured. He listened to our concerns and empathized and helped create solutions. Regardless of our dotted line, I never felt subordinate to him. I felt like a partner. Corporate manuals recommended us to talk to and about employees and coworkers as "teammates," almost as if it were part of some act. With James you actually were part of his team, and he was the quarterback. He could have written the book.

He was the real thing, genuine. He was just a few years older than I was with thick black hair and a cool, calm way about him that was contagious. He put you at ease in his presence. He was a great leader and a friend of mine. He would even try to help me later on when I was no longer in his branch and began uncovering fraud. But there was only so much he could do.

Chapter 12

I couldn't have had a better introduction to a new bank than at Carle Place working for a guy like James Duggan. Once I got settled into the routine of life as the SBRM, we ran like a well-oiled machine. I would head out all over Nassau meeting with clients, learning about their businesses, and uncovering their needs then making sure their needs were met. I'd always hand them an extra business card and say, "If you're happy with me, please tell a friend." They often did. I also met with prospects looking to bring in new business. I usually researched prospects and their industries before meeting with them for the first time. They appreciated my being well informed.

The research would occasionally lead me to decide that I'd prefer not to do business with them. I had one prospect looking to refinance a strip shopping center in an established upscale town. He owned and occupied a well-known restaurant in 40 percent of the space. The remainder of the space in the very well-kept building was fully occupied by offices and stores with long-term triple-net leases. The building was worth about $1,500,000, and his loan request was for 50 percent of the value or $750,000. He would have more than sufficient cash flow to support the repayment of the new loan. I looked at buildings in the area and checked out ratings of his restaurant. His financials looked fine. But with one search on Google, I came to learn that he was under indictment for setting fire to the building occupied by his competition down the block.

Sometimes the checking was my least favorite part of the job because it called for me to be suspicious and verify everything. Sometimes my research was as simple as going to the location to make sure the business existed, and there's hardly any more insulting behavior than to imply someone's legitimate business doesn't actually exist. However, like I mentioned, at Carle Place I personally dealt with few instances of outright fraud. But there was one case of fraud I was familiar with.

The business specialist on our team, Carmen Espanida, had a huge following of mortgage brokers. As the SBRM, I handled business clients with borrowing needs of $250,000 to $3,000,000. The business specialist handled lesser amounts, and when the client's borrowing needs grew to over the $3,000,000 amount, the client would be handled by an officer in our Middle Market Group. However, as I stressed before, we worked as a team, and relationship manager changes were supposed to be seamless to the clients. Carmen was technically working in a position subordinate to mine, but she reported to her own segment leader and to James. However, the fact that she did not report to me did not mean I could not be concerned if I suspected questionable behavior. I did pay attention.

I noticed that she never "held funds" on any checks. She regularly approved checks deposited by clients and made them "immediately available." Just on its face it was clear to me that this was at least non-standard bank policy or practice. I knew I must bring this up to James, but he was not concerned. Anyone who has had a checking account knows that if you deposit a check, the bank will make available a portion of the funds but you have to wait for the check to clear the paying bank. And if some of the funds or all of the funds are made immediately available to the payee and the check is then returned by the paying bank (say for insufficient funds, forgery, or endorsement) the depositor owes that money back to the depository bank. Simple. The practice of making funds immediately available is risky and by policy typically only done if the check is a government check or a cashier's check.

When I asked James about it, he said, "No, she's fine, she knows what she's doing."

But everything wasn't fine. I always wondered about this with regard to James; why he didn't press her a little harder? Her behavior was loose, to say the least.

The police came for her in late September of 2008. She had signed fraudulent account documents for clients while she worked at Chase just a little over a year before. She was found guilty and released with a suspended sentence, but the message was clear. Carmen had been a participant in questionable mortgage lending practices. The banks in the past ten years had wholesale arms that did the underwriting and funding of mortgage loans that were brought to them by mortgage brokers. There were plenty of ways to defraud the lender: straw buyer, inflated income, fakes tax returns, inflated appraisals, and false statements of sources of down payments, and so on and so on. Earlier in 2008, Carmen had received a top sales performance award from HSBC, and at a joint meeting of our business specialists and BRMs she was praised by our segment leaders. She got some nice incentives and a dream vacation to Hawaii. We all clapped for her. We were supposed to be motivated by her success. But as her past misdeeds came to light, the message was not so motivational to some of our clients, who heard about how she was arrested for signing false documents.

Banks are funny institutions that can be damaged by a whisper. At the slightest talk of fraud, customers can get nervous and pull their accounts or refuse to sign up. It's also a tactic of other business reps to raise awareness of infractions: "Did you hear so-and-so got arrested for signing false documents over at HSBC Carle Place? Yeah, it's a shame. Things seem to have gone downhill over there."

We faced this problem immediately after Carmen's arrest. When I sat with clients new and old, there was hardly one who didn't bring up the story of Carmen and what we were doing to ensure that it wasn't happening again. I would always point out that she hadn't actually accomplished her crimes at our bank, but it didn't matter. We hired her and that was enough; and besides, a lot of her same clients from Chase followed her to HSBC. Most customers assumed we knew and just turned a blind eye; either that or we were stupid. It was a hard bind to be in. It wasn't like a bank run where customers were worried about losing their money by banking with us, but they got the sense that different branches could rot like fruit on the vine and it was best to stay away from those branches. In this assumption, they were absolutely correct—only I couldn't say this at the time. But in comparison to branches I would soon encounter, Carle Place was pristine.

Aside from James's momentary lapse of judgment regarding Carmen, he ran a strong office. He created a competitive environment that helped me drive even harder than I had before. I was acquiring more clients than I ever had. In many ways I simply went off my old book of clients from the credit union and the contacts I had amassed, but several times, as with the lawyer, I would find clients cold. I would have acquired even more business if it hadn't been for Carmen and her shenanigans. Doing PR and damage control because of her fraud cost me plenty of time and energy.

My proudest moment from my first ten months at the Carle Place branch was when I had a billionaire hedge fund manager on the line. He had nearly forty billion in assets under his management. What was funny about him was that when I think forty billion, I think fancy cars, slick demeanor, and intolerable attitude. But if you saw this guy, you would never have guessed that he controlled forty *thousand* dollars, let alone the billions people entrusted him with. Even his office was a little messy, which really made me wonder what type of people would give him their life's savings, but they did, and apparently he did very well by them. I guess he started in a middle-sized Wall Street firm and after a few years went out on his own. When he had some good calls, people took notice, and he started to get enough business to set up a shop. He went out on the Island because he no longer wanted the city pressure. And I think he liked the idea of waking up and driving just a few minutes with no traffic to a small village office where he had a receptionist and a small but efficient staff. Mostly I think he just kept apace of the world from home, and as he continued to make the right calls almost without fail throughout 2008 and 2009, he continued to land big clients. I heard about him through a friend of mine who'd met him at a dinner, and I simply knocked on his office door one day.

That's all it took to get the ball rolling, but a client of his size needed to be brought in by upper management. He was also asking for a few compensations that I didn't have the authorization to give. Regardless of whether I finally landed him as a client, the fact that I got him to the table a few months after starting the job made people at the bank take notice.

James joked to me that I would soon have his job if I kept moving like that. "I'm going to have to sabotage you." But he was actually happy for me. Sometimes competitive environments can go too far and the sprit of contest turns into bloodletting and petty rivalry, but at Carle Place working under James Duggan, it never existed. He was just happy for the branch to do well, the same way a coach wants his players to win and doesn't handicap them for some crazy reason.

Under this type of environment, we were able to make the Carle Place branch the number-one branch in Nassau. Regional success may not seem like much, but this was Nassau County, home to some of the wealthiest people in the world, and I was helping to push our business to the number-one spot in the county. The number-one spot in the region, on the other hand, was held by the East Northport branch, whose numbers were so far and away bigger that there was some curiosity if not suspicion about how they were bringing in such huge numbers. But this little fact didn't concern me yet.

Chapter 13

I couldn't have expected a better year. I was making nearly triple the money I had at the credit union, and I was enjoying what I did—not to mention that as the economy slipped into recession, I only felt more and more comfortable in my decision to move to HSBC.

Under James Duggan, I also had free rein. I was his right-hand man and had access to all the files he did. We worked together both creating new accounts and keeping the ones we already had. I've learned that while money can make someone happy for a time, what really makes you happy is a having a place in the world and doing something you love. But finding that place can be tough. Here I had this very thing. I belonged.

Little did I know it was all about to come apart. Bill Fargus was the BRM and SBRM's segment leader for Nassau and Suffolk counties out of the Melville office. He had joined HSBC in October of 2007. That was when HSBC was working on an initiative to beef up the business-specialist and business-relationship-manager staff. HSBC was gearing up to aggressively grow their business relationships both on the deposit and loan sides. From those business relationships, they would garner the personal deposit relationships and investments of the business owners. Bill was a good man, and James only had good things to say about him. Bill was a good leader in every sense of the word. He set firm yet realistic expectations. He encouraged sharing of plans and ideas at our team meetings. He also enjoyed going out on business calls with the BRMs and SBRMs. He liked to work with us on pre-call planning, and then he'd ask us to critique ourselves after a call. This practice may seem to be one for the inexperienced—it was not. It kept us at our best. Bill was conversational, not confrontational, and to the experienced team he had it was an approach that worked. He was respectful and earned respect in return.

Looking back, maybe there were indications that trouble was heading our way. Maybe it was the kind of trouble that makes people lose the secure feeling about their jobs. The kind of feeling that may lead them to behave poorly or make bad decisions. There had been an employee survey conducted on a regional level, and the purpose was "to make HSBC the 'Best Place to Work.'" There were focus groups to analyze our responses and develop a plan.

We were given the results, and the topics that received the most attention were these: promote the best people; deal appropriately with poor performance; maintain honest, open, two-way communication;

show employees that their contributions are valued; and provide opportunity for growth and development. The timing of the questionnaire now strikes me as odd. And some of the results, like maintaining honest, open, two-way communication ring even more truly as a concern now. Employees certainly felt their work environment was less than honest then. Did someone at the regional level already know the type of culture that had become ensconced?

Another indication that something was amiss was the last minute cancellation of our scheduled two-day "Business Banking Leadership Conference." All of the SBRMs and BRMs were looking forward to this time together upstate New York, planning, strategizing, building teamwork, sharing ideas, and all of the great happy stuff that comes with having a great job with a great company. There was no explanation, just an e-mail to let us know the meeting was canceled. Most of us figured it was to save money. We were advised that we could read through the presentation slide show if we cared to. It was made available to us on the report retrieval program on our computers.

Then seemingly out of nowhere toward the end of 2008, Bill Fargus told us he had resigned indicating something like "the job cannot get done the way I want to do it, and I cannot do the job the way senior management wants it done…so it is in the interest of all…leaving on good terms." He stuck around for several weeks to wrap things up. We were all sure that it was more a case of "quit or you'll be let go," but he was a gentleman and never said that.

There had been a reshuffling of senior management. Joseph Morabito was the senior vice president in charge of the Nassau County branches, and Sanja Malhotra was in charge of Suffolk. But then there was a consolidation at the top by the corporate office in an effort to cut waste and pull in more profit. In this move they decided that Morabito and his position were no longer necessary, and so they gave him his walking papers.

Morabito was a great guy, whom I knew well. He talked straight and ran an upright team. You always knew where you stood and what to expect when he was involved. But now Malhotra was in charge of all Long Island. His title didn't change, but his geographic reach certainly did, and his responsibilities doubled, at least. The differences in his leadership style were also apparent immediately in that the directives that came down from him were opaque. In other words, whenever James Duggan spoke with him, there would always be a lot of room for interpretation in what he was supposed to do.

Unfortunately, you come across this style too often in senior management. I believe it's a strategy for corporate survival that some use to get by. You don't say what you mean, and you don't give directions that can be directly interpreted and traced back to you whenever you can avoid it. "Oh the buck stops over there." It's a way to shirk responsibility, because if you're not direct, or at least not very clear, you can always pass the buck down the line. "I never directed you to do that; all I said was that I wanted these results." Ivan used to always say that "shit flows downhill," and this type of leadership gets it flowing faster. It's a bad way of doing business, but it's there.

Malhotra also had another trait that just irritated me and which I bring up because I think it was linked to his pass-the-buck command style. He always smiled and held his hands together, "Oh that is great. It is great. Things are very good. You are doing so well." And this right before he took some action against you. His happiness was an act to get people on his side. He was outwardly mild mannered. Nobody I ever spoke with felt that he didn't like them. He wanted people to think of him as a great guy who was on your side. Even if you disagreed with him, he had little to say in response. He left you with the feeling that he agreed with you. But you would find out later from someone else, one of his puppets, that he did not agree with you at all, leaving you without the dignity of a conversation. He had a way to push you to do things in an entirely asymmetrical way that would be difficult to trace back to his words.

When Morabito was terminated and Malhotra was brought in, Bill Fargus tendered his resignation as the section leader in Melville. This was definitely Malhotra's call. The way we knew for sure, though Bill said nothing, was by how under-the-radar it was. When Morabito fired someone, you knew he did it, and also why he had done it. But this was quiet and complicated, which bore all the marks of Malhotra.

Whatever the reason was for the shakeup, and why certain people were terminated over others remained a secret. The moment Bill was gone, a position opened for immediate hiring. James Duggan was the number-one candidate. He immediately stepped into the position on a temporary basis even before being offered it because he was needed.

James had worked inside HSBC for over twenty years and was held in high esteem. He understood every aspect of the business development from the ground up, so he was the natural choice. In fact, there was no better candidate for the job. One of the other senior business relationship managers said to me, "I would try for that position but there's no point; Duggan's got it locked up." She was right; he did have it locked up. And as his duties shifted, so my duties also shifted to encompass what he had been doing. This arrangement worked fine. I knew how to do his job, and could take on the tasks he had accomplished. I had often filled in for him whenever he was out, and so the additional responsibilities were easy; in fact, I liked the addition to my responsibilities for the time being.

But James wasn't thrilled in his new assignment as segment leader. While he was perfectly competent doing the job, it called for him to be in the office for long hours—far more than James, as a family man, cared to spend at the office. "It's not something I like very much," he said. "I've worked enough years that I don't need to prove anything." I empathized with him. When I saw the long hours he was working, I didn't envy him. He also wasn't comfortable in the position. It wasn't his niche, so to speak.

So when he was asked finally to take the position permanently, he declined the offer. This meant that corporate had to look for someone else to fill his place. At first when I heard that he was remaining in the same capacity at Carle Place, I was excited because it meant that our group would remain together. We were comfortable, and I hated to see it dissolve so quickly. In the corporate world you can often get stuck working in difficult situations with people who are not cooperative. When you have a good thing, you hate to see it go.

But before James returned, he had bad news. He knew who they had hired to take his place, and he didn't like it. "If I knew they were going to hire him, I would have kept that position," he told me one afternoon at lunch. "He's a problem. I've know him for a while. He's real bitter. They brought him in from WaMu; I think he was canned when Chase took over."

"That's great news," I said.

"Yeah well, you wouldn't want me to lie to you. Things are probably going to get a lot more complicated now. You've got to walk on eggshells around the guy."

James couldn't have known just how complicated my world was really going to get. The man we were talking about was Mitchell K. Janson. His story was that he had worked for Chase Bank as a manager until he was let go. Then he moved over to Washington Mutual, but when Chase bought WaMu he was let go again. I don't know why they brought him over to HSBC after a performance record like that, and it's not to say that people don't deserve more than one chance, but this guy was really a prickly man who probably would have been better off with less responsibility. He probably

101

aced the interview or was sized up to be a good puppet/hatchet man. I think his problem was that he didn't believe in human chemistry. It wasn't even that he could only see the numbers; that would have been an acceptable trait in a boss. He could only see his own ideas. The whole notion of a team and even real camaraderie on the job was alien to him. He was a narcissist with a steamroller personality. Neither quality makes for great teamwork.

At our first team meeting, he did all the talking and lots of it. He was like a "radio," with just one way of communication. He mostly set out his rules, his expectations, and his demands. He talked to us like we were trainees; I'd say our average experience was upwards of twenty years. The SBRMs and BRMs were educated, experienced, and dedicated. It was actually funny when he lectured us on being on time and having our shoes shined. His next big idea was that we'd all be moving our offices to Melville, and we'd be expected there every day. Now, we all had from one to seven branches that we covered, but our portfolios were similar in number of accounts and dollars managed. We all also actively participated in the business communities in our territories, such as networking groups, chambers, and service groups, and we all served in at least one charitable organization. You could say we spent a lot of time on the road. This plan to check in at Melville, where his office was, each day, was a control issue. He was trying to sell us on the idea of teamwork and camaraderie, but we already had that. Most of us helped one another out on a regular basis.

One of Janson's next moves was to change up the branches that the SBRMs and BRMs covered. There was much discussion on this topic, and things were heated. It takes a long while to become known and respected in a community, and each of us had done it quite well. It appeared that Janson's first plan was thrown together by throwing all the names of the branches into a hat and pulling our names out of another hat to match us up. It made no sense. And we had no say in the matter.

In early March, sixty employees in Nassau and Suffolk were laid off. Two were SBRMs—a hard hit since we were already stretched thin. One of our most senior guys and a top performer had already quit. Shortly after the layoff, two more were let go.

It was in this turmoil late one Friday afternoon that I was informed I was going to be transferred out of the Carle Place Branch. It was late March 2009. By the end of that month, I was the SBRM for seven branches scattered from just shy of the east end of Long Island in Suffolk County back west all the way to Manhattan. A few of these branches had grown large enough that they were badly in need of an SBRM to cover more of their customers. But these SBRMs should have been brought in from around the branch's local area to ensure that the person already had a book of clients and knew the territory. This would have been the standard procedure. But what Janson did instead was to take me from Carle Place and designate me the SBRM of the seven scattered branches that were without one. It was a bad idea because it automatically reduced the face time I would have with individual clients. It also placed me into in at least four or five territories where I had no history or connection. Not all of the branches needed an SBRM; they simply did not have the business yet to justify it. They did need the SBRM to grow new, larger business, but that was a different story, and it was Jansen's call.

"We need someone in those branches. They don't have the slot filled," he said when I asked him about it on a Monday morning. "And you're it."

I was upset by this: "All of my clients are in this area; I've maintained a book here for years. I'm only going to continue to grow that book. The territory is also too large for one person. Why would you put one person in charge of all of them? It's too spread out."

But I should never have said that. I had been working with James too long and had gotten into the habit of actually discussing the plans we would undertake. I was also in the position of normally, if not agreeing, at least understanding the move that James was going to make, but this was ridiculous.

He replied to me: "It's none of your business. Do your fucking job. Have a nice day."

He looked crazed from across the desk. His eyes were wild. I just nodded and walked out. Happy Monday to you, too, I thought. I wasn't sure what else to do. I had been in banking all my life and had never been talked to like that before. We were certainly in new territory.

I didn't protest any further at that moment. You can't really argue with the people above you in a corporation, especially when they are so belligerent. I was obviously not going to get anywhere with him. But I had to work with him. I went to James, naturally, who already knew all about the move and was entirely against it. He went to Janson and told him that he needed me where I was in Carle Place. He told Janson that he didn't want to be short-handed, and that I was literally his right-hand man bringing in and keeping most of the business we had.

"I tried, John," he said, "I told him that you were the reason we made Carle Place number one. If I lose you I lose a big part of my team. But he didn't care. He told me that I would have to retrain someone else. 'We need him over there,' he said, and that was pretty much the end of the conversation. He's not really interested in the way things are or what other people think; he's sure he's right, and he's going to prove it. The guy's like a wrecking ball."

Chapter 14

"But why do you have to go?" It was early in the morning, and my wife wanted to know why I had to accept the change Janson had imposed. "There has to be something you can do. I mean, they recruited you at Carle Place based on your book, and now this guy comes in and just does whatever he wants. It makes no sense."

"Yeah, well, even Duggan couldn't reason with him. It's only one way with this guy."

"Go over his head."

"Corporate wouldn't touch it with a ten-foot pole. They put the guy in to shake things up, and that's what he's doing. I doubt they'd care much about what I have to say."

It was time for me to get to work with the new branches I had been assigned to. I could complain as much as I wanted, but no one was going to listen. And so I packed my stuff up from the Carle Place branch and got prepared for the new office over in Melville.

The staff at Carle Place had heard about the SBRM changes. Adel, who was a business-banking specialist, turned to me as I left and said, "It's a shame." She had worked banking since before I was in high school. "There's no telling where they're liable to transfer anyone now. They run this place from Shanghai; how the hell do they know what's going on?"

What Adel said was how most other people felt around the office, except no one would speak about it openly. Among the many games people play in corporations is whack-a-mole. Unlike the arcade, however, the corporate version has players on both sides. As an employee, your job is to stick your head above ground only as long as absolutely necessary. Management's job is to give those people who keep their heads above ground for too long a good whack. And so, while most people would privately voice their opinion to me, no one would or could go on record, except James, for fear they would just get whacked. It's also funny how mafia terminology so readily lends itself to the corporate world. One of the things I would come to learn working at HSBC was how closely linked and incestuous these two worlds actually are. But that was just around the corner.

For now I was stuck in between offices. The closest thing to a personal office that I had was my cubicle at corporate in Melville, but I spent far more time in my car than anywhere else. And even after the change of responsibilities, I still had to spend a great deal of my time helping out the new guy who had been made SBRM in Carle Place. And this is what I never understood: by moving me, not only were a new set of branches underserviced by an SBRM who didn't know the territory, but then an already-settled branch was thrown into disarray because I was removed and a new guy was in training.

For the next few months, I was working eighteen-hour days, and I was encountering difficulty in aligning with some of my new branches. In a few areas, branch managers were perfectly happy with the way things were and didn't want to deal with me. One BM out in Ronkonkoma—and yes, I was back where I had started in college—told me to just leave him alone. "Look, I know you're doing your job, and I heard about how and why they put you here, so I'm with you, I really am. I know what it's like, and I'm sure you're none too happy about it. But not for nothing, you don't know the territory, you don't have a book here, you got no history. The way this is going to have to work is that I keep doing what I was doing, and call you when I need you. This will be easier for both of us."

I went along with him on this because I didn't want to get off on the wrong foot to begin with. And besides, he was right; I needed him to begin with, and if this was how he wanted to go, I would have to follow his lead for the time being. Later I could get the lay of the land and make a few connections with clients. Otherwise, if the manager and SBRM didn't get along, nothing good would come of it. The last thing we needed in a lousy economy, working short staffed everywhere, was to wind up in a tug-of-war over clients and territory.

All in all, the transition went smoothly in the other offices. A few of them had been without an SBRM when they really needed one, and so even though I was over-stretched and had no history or contacts in their area, they embraced me and gave me whatever assistance I needed to bring in new business and work with their current clients.

But that still left me with Carle Place, where they had brought in a new SBRM, Bob Cicero, who really had no business doing this job at all. I don't know where they found him, but he just didn't grasp the basics of what his clients needed. What this led to was that after he had pissed them off enough, they called me. And when they called me, James would also call me.

I was doing my best to transition from the Carle Place book to the new accounts Janson had assigned to me. But it was made more complicated because my clients didn't want to stop using me. A few of my former clients switched branches in order to keep me as their relationship manager. I really tried to stop that from happening. It's just bad practice. It hurt the balances of the Carle Place office, which was quickly losing its number-one status. Cicero wasn't bringing in new clients either, so Carle Place was suddenly shrinking at both ends. While I still had to maintain ties with that branch, I was simultaneously forging new relationships all over the island.

I practically lived in my car. I reluctantly had to switch my phone to voice mail for periods during the day just to have the time to get client files and loan requests in proper order and submitted. The phone was on constantly while I was driving. I'd be driving, looking at my GPS to figure out where I was, eating my lunch, and talking with a client. There was no peace. My life was suddenly gone. On top of that, Janson, fearless leader that he was, liked to call his employees at all hours of the night. After I got a call from him at three a.m. interrogating me about why the Ronkonkoma branch was lagging, I never left my phone on again after ten p.m. Thank God the guy didn't have my home number. I don't even want to imagine what my wife would have had to say to him should she have picked up a three a.m. call. For a little while, I thought he just had it out for me, until I heard from James that Janson had called him at the same hour on a few occasions.

This new career move I had chosen had suddenly begun to look like the wrong move. But I was sure there would be light at the end of the tunnel. When my wife would say to me, "I don't even see you anymore," I'd respond that the hardest part would be over in six months. I thought that after the transition and when I'd made some contacts, things would get easier. I thought all I had to do was to build up a rapport with the clients and get Cicero on his feet, and everything would return to the way it had been. Little did I know what was really coming around the corner, and if I could only have seen what I was getting into with some of the new branches and what it would expose me to, I would have gotten out. I would have asked for a transfer, or I would have asked for my old job back at the credit union. Under no circumstances would I have continued working for HSBC and within its culture. It's as simple as that. But I couldn't have known these things then.

Chapter 15

East Northport was the beginning of a new assignment and the end of my tolerance for what I had been assigned to do. And yet it was such a charming area. Northport and East Northport together form one of the larger communities by population on the North Shore. On Long Island, most of the people, as you'd imagine, are concentrated on the western end of the island by Manhattan. The densest parts of the island radiate out from there, but generally southern and central areas are far more populated. In fact, the North Shore, in places, still has the Gilded Age feel to it, with expansive lawns and dense oak woods. East Northport was no different.

Since I lived out of my car, I spent a lot of time evaluating different areas based on what I could gather of them from the highway or whatever other main roads I was on. I'd make notes of areas where there would likely be a good target for cold calls. I'd pick out well-kept professional office parks or industrial condos. I recall my first drive up to the Northport area to visit my new branch. It had been a while since I was up on the North Shore. I had a pleasant and relaxed feeling as I enjoyed the country drive. Northport is a beautiful old community settled around Cow Harbor. It was farm country and then a wood shipbuilding town. Its population grew quickly in the early nineteen hundreds when shops, trains, and trolleys served the residents. The town has kept its old charm.

At times, even when the pressure was high and I had schedules to keep, I would work my lunch in as part of a longer drive. On these lunches I would take the scenic route and eat while I drove. I liked to find the hidden places on the Island I had never seen before. I still had the sense, even from when I was a kid living at the scrapyard, that Long Island was the hub of the world, at least the Eastern Seaboard, and I loved to explore it. These explorations allowed me time to relax my mind and think job-related issues over in a less pressured, more leisurely environment.

The first time I drove up to the East Northport office, I had a meeting with the branch manager, Anjali Indira. Her branch had outperformed the Carle Place Branch where I had been posted, but as they were in Suffolk we hadn't been rated against her, although we certainly knew what she had been doing, or at least how good her numbers had been. As I've mentioned, there was a lot of speculation about what caused this. But the answer was usually that, with all the wealth up on the North Shore, and fewer people, she had landed a couple of huge accounts which had thrust her figures over the top.

On the South Shore, basically south of the Southern State Parkway, there were more people and a higher concentration of business so you could scrabble together more accounts and more middle to high balance accounts. But if you landed a billionaire or two and only landed a fraction of the business, you could be better off. The interesting part about Anjali's branch, though, wasn't that she was outperforming everyone else; it was by how much she had been outperforming every other branch on the Island, and possibly the whole North American segment.

I had been investigating fraud my entire career in banking. Anytime we went into another credit union and one of its branches had been vastly outperforming its other branches, I knew right off the bat that it was likely someone was committing fraud—though not always. But for some reason it didn't strike me that any of HSBC's branches would be engaged in fraud in this same way.

I guess the reason was that there was a lot less oversight in a small credit union, in that there was often no ruling corporate office that could make decisions from on high. In this system, if the union had only three or four offices, or less, one branch could be corrupt; and also if that manger had enough power among the others, he could create an adequate screen or bully the other members to hide his fraud.

But in a major corporation, with oversight and auditors checking the numbers at every level, and with the total amount of money that the bank saw, no one branch could get a leg up to create an adequate screen to hide its fraud behind. But this just shows how little

I knew about fraud at this level, where all of these systems can themselves be turned into a screen.

Yet I wasn't thinking about any of this on my car ride up to East Northport. It was late April, but there was still a bitter chill in the air. I've always hated the cold. But it was mostly the oak trees on my mind as I drove through Dix Hills and Elwood, and then through a long stretch of narrow, twisting road. At a point I was lost and had to turn back. The GPS had me moving in circles, or actually, squares: "Turn left, turn left, turn left."

I got myself headed in the right direction and went up to East Northport to meet with Anjali. She had been so pleasant on the phone when I told her I was coming up to see her branch and to meet with her. I was surprised. Several of the branch managers I had been assigned to, while they admitted needing an SBRM, wanted to have the choice of who their SBRM would be. And if the decision had to come down from the district level, they at least wanted the person to be familiar with the area. But when I was imposed on them from Carle Place without a single client in the area and having never done business there, some of them were a little less than welcoming.

But Anjali was cordial on the phone, and even seemed open to my presence. Naturally when I arrived I was expecting to have a warm welcome. I walked in through the doors a few minutes before one o'clock, our scheduled meeting time.

"Oh, I'm sorry she had to step out. She should be back a little after one," the woman who came out to greet me said.

With that we were off to a bad start, but I could put it behind me. Surely there are instances where branch managers are called away unexpectedly. It comes with the job. But when she returned about an hour late for our meeting, she was not happy to see me. She scowled at me when she saw me through the glass partition that separated her waiting area from the rest of the bank.

"Come in," she said. She hadn't bothered to apologize for keeping me. I took her attitude with a grain of salt and suggested that we plan some joint calls with some of her preferred clients. These were existing clients that were put into my portfolio based on specific criteria. They wanted me to develop relationships with the business she had acquired over the last year or so in order to deepen their loyalty to us. I would work toward building the relationships with the older customers over time or as it became necessary. My first priority would be reviewing the new clients' files and learning about their business and their industries. This was standard practice. However, gaining access to these clients would be easier said than done. Most of the deposit and loan information was available to me through the computer system, and there was very little I could not access on the system. But rather than searching through the data alone, it's always best to get the heads up from the BM—just a feeling about the client, who they are, what they want, and how they started their business can be great intel to have. The manager can help you to see the things you wouldn't get from the numbers. In some instances, the balances can be large with little activity. These "insight" tips can mean you don't waste time uncovering a client's needs.

But this wasn't to be. Anjali looked at me and said, "I'm not going to share my clients with you." Other branch managers hadn't wanted to deal with me, but none had outright declined to allow me to know about their clients. No manager had refused to discuss them with me. I was there to bring in more business for her branch. I was supposed to be a part of her "team." It made no sense.

"I don't understand. Why won't you let me see them?"

"What's there not to understand?" She was looking right at me now across the desk. "You'll see the clients and the papers that I give you to look at. You're not going to come into my branch with some fucking list from Janson at Melville and expect me to show you all of my clients. I've been handling this branch fine by myself, and by myself I took it to number one; now I don't want some guy, and no offence to you personally, but some guy from Carle Place taking over the business here. I'll call you when I put together some clients to review."

That was that. I left the branch and returned to the parking lot. I was livid, but there was only so much I could do. If I was rude to her, she could try to make my life even harder. I sat for a few minutes while the pulsing in my neck turned to normal. Since Janson was serious and crystal clear about my remaining in as the SBRM over these branches, I knew I had better not cause any more trouble than there already was.

Whatever the reason for her reluctance to talk to me, there was nothing I could do about it now. I drove to Melville and got in to see Janson face to face. I waited a few minutes outside of his office before he came out for me.

"John, how are you?"

"Well, I've been better. I just met with the BM for East Northport."

"Anjali Indira?"

"She wouldn't talk to me at all. First she made me wait an hour."

"Did you say anything to piss her off?"

"Of course I didn't. I've been talking to these BMs all over the Island; I haven't had anyone treat me like this. And I didn't even get a chance to talk. She plain came out and said, 'you're only gonna see the clients that I show you.' What the hell can I do with that? How do I work with a hostile branch?"

He thought for a moment and said, "Whatever she wants, give it to her, just give it to her, John."

"What?"

"Just deal with her. I'm not getting involved with her branch right away like that."

"But I'm involved with her branch right now, and she doesn't want me there."

"Just deal with her on a slow basis. Do what you can through the computer on your own."

I said good-bye and left. How the hell was I going to deal with her on a "slow basis?" I didn't even know what that meant. If I was going to develop and expand business relationships and manage the portfolios of business clients, and I was being judged on that performance, I couldn't very well do it if I didn't have any access to those clients. But it was obvious that he didn't want to hear what I had to say. I knew he didn't care either.

Chapter 16

I scheduled time on my calendar for a follow-up visit to East Northport the next week. I kept up the hope that I would reconnect with Anjali on better terms. Janson had made it clear that he wasn't going to give me any support on the matter. Whatever he meant by "going slow," I was sure it didn't include my avoiding her office. If she was going to get comfortable with me then she was going to have to see me. Maybe then she would allow me to do my job. But the real problem was that she wouldn't allow me to have access to any of her clients directly through her, and that's what I had to remedy, especially if I was going to be judged on my performance here.

As I walked into the branch, I was cheerfully greeted by Janice, whom I had first met at the Carle Place branch. We had become better acquainted participating in various HSBC functions during the last year. Janice Martin was in her early fifties and was now the branch operations manager in East Northport. She had been in banking since she graduated college. She was an honest, experienced lady who knew the lay of the land, and she had a good sense of humor, which was becoming a rarity at work these days. Not only that, but she was friendly and easy to talk to. This morning the typical coworker exchange began: "How's it going?" "You getting sick of this place yet?" "Well, I guess you didn't win the lottery since you're still here."

But then she asked me, "Has she let you see them?" She was referring to Anjali's clients. I guess news spread fast.

"No."

"Well, don't be surprised if she keeps fighting you on it."

But she wouldn't tell me why. When I pressed her, she just smiled a sort of knowing smile. But she wouldn't expand on what she meant and I didn't want to piss her off. I wanted to mull over what she'd said and figure out what she meant.

Janice went back to work, and I made a few phone calls to the clients from other branches that actually appreciated working with me. While on the phone, one client recommended I contact an acquaintance of his. I did, and by the end of the day I had picked up a new client. Most of the time, I would bring in new business clients this way. Nothing is better than a recommendation from a satisfied customer. One would lead to another and so on and so on—like the old shampoo commercial. There has been a saying in banking for years. If a client has a bad experience, they tell ten people; if they have a good experience, they tell two. If you can be the banker that makes their experience great, well, do the math; you'll do well with referrals. I have found also that clients like to be the ones who discover and share information with their colleagues, friends, and family; people are often excited by the idea of turning a friend onto something new or better.

After about an hour on the phone, I filled contacts into my "Lotus Book," which at that time was the relationship managers' new tracking "tool." Anjali came out of her office and began to talk with me, but it was obvious that her mind was somewhere else. She seemed stressed out and kept trailing off. When I would pick up on a topic, she'd quickly lose interest and change the subject entirely. I was well aware of the fact that I was sitting with a BM who was totally belligerent and that our last meeting was horrible. I let her continue to lead the conversation. For the moment I would just try to make her comfortable with me on the off chance that she was withholding because she was jealous.

Then she asked what I guessed was the reason she had come over to my desk in the first place.

"You're a notary, right?"

"You know I am."

"Well, I need you to notarize a signature on the documents for a small loan for me. It's for my husband and me, I'm almost embarrassed to ask like this. But it's already been through the underwriter."

"Sure, just send me over the paperwork," I said.

"Why do you need to see the papers? I just told you it was already through the underwriter."

"Excuse me. Of course I need to see the papers. And they need to be signed in my presence."

"This is not the way to make friends."

I sighed openly. If I'd been in charge she'd be out on her ass. She was asking me to compromise myself on the basis of what she thought was her position over me.

She stomped off to her office. I looked over my shoulder, and Janice was shaking her head at me in a sarcastic manner. She smiled at me wryly. I returned the sentiment with my own smile. I was apprehensive. I hadn't wanted to get Anjali angry or to get angry myself, but here we were. Now I was sure she'd make my life even more difficult. I had only been at this new position a few weeks, and things weren't looking any better.

Anjali suddenly reappeared at my desk with an empty folder in one hand and loan paperwork in the other. She tossed the documents onto my desk. They were paper clipped together, opened to the notary's section. I wasn't pleased. I slowly picked up the stack of papers and reviewed them, peeling back one page at a time like a banana. She stood over my shoulder the entire time. When I was satisfied they were in order, I stood, reached into my pocket for my car keys, and headed toward the door.

"Where are you going?" she demanded.

"Out to my car, where my stamp and seal are locked for safekeeping. I don't just carry the stamp in my briefcase."

Anjali smirked at me as I walked out the door. Janice didn't look up at all. She kept her head down in her small cubicle, but I imagined that she was laughing to herself. I climbed into my office on wheels and poked through my glove box for the stamp, making a mental note to clean this car later on. I found the stamp in the navy box it came in, and I returned to my desk and stamped and signed the document. It was as simple as that. Anjali went back behind her glass wall without thanking me. I thought about striking up a conversation about "our" clients again, but I thought that might be in poor taste at the moment. Based on the aspects of her personality that she had shown me so far, I figured that she might think I was trying to force the issue, that I thought I was one up on her because I'd notarized her signature. It was crazy that I had to think in circles to figure out how to work with her. I had been making some progress on my own doing research on the Customer Information System. It was difficult because the computer system's information and the accessing of it were time-consuming and incomplete. But I had plenty of experience at investigating from my work at the credit union and was able in time to cull out some good information.

The computer research I had to undertake, instead of her tacit help, might help to explain why I began to find aberrations so quickly. Had Anjali sent me around to her major clients, then I wouldn't have had to poke around on the computer. In addition, I wouldn't have begun to discover a disturbing trend at the East Northport branch as I was now doing. My suspicions were just an impression so far. I also knew that such impressions often grew with more evidence.

A few days later, I returned to East Northport after making the rounds of other branches and their clients and some prospects. I also met with the BRM for some of the Nassau Branches, Karthic Arumugum. I walked in through the glass lobby and past the ATMs, and then the inside lobby doors and saw Janice sitting at her desk. By the look and nod she gave me when I came through the door it was obvious she wanted to talk with me.

"Did you notarize it?" she asked

"Yeah, everything was fine."

"Well, there's a business banking specialist in the office who had her notary duplicated by Anjali a few months back," she said.

"What?"

"She notarized something, and then her notary started to show up on documents she never saw and loans she didn't know about."

"No? Who?"

"She's not in today," Janice said. "Angela Martin?"

"Martin?" I asked?

"No relation to me," she said.

"What happened?"

She didn't respond right away. Then she said, "Just be careful."

And so I was, but how could I be careful with that? When a manager in a corporation asks you to do something reasonable which is neither against the law nor against the company policy, you do it. If you don't you get reprimanded.

"What else?" I asked her.

"This branch isn't like you expect. She'll use you."

Anjali was looking at us then through the glass partition. We both saw her. Janice hung around at the edge of the desk I sat at for a few moments more, then she smiled and went back to her work. I thought a lot of things in the few minutes after Janice told me about the forged notary stamps, but the one thing I kept coming back to was the concern that I wasn't safe anymore.

At the credit union, we had a team, and I knew who was on it. But now suddenly I realized I could get sacked by my own players with very little warning. If there was an enemy, then it was all around me. I pushed that sort of paranoia away immediately, though. I couldn't live like that, and I didn't want to entertain the conclusions I was drawing. But I did begin to think that my career had now gone from investigating crooked banks to working in one, and I would conduct myself accordingly.

Chapter 17

Our Commack office was another of my new assignments. The town of Commack was six miles or so southeast of East Northport. While Commack didn't have the historic waterfront charm, it had its share of wealthy individual clients, retailers, professionals, and some light industry. It had potential for me, but my first time at the branch was informative for all the wrong reasons. Just like at East Northport, the branch manager didn't want to have anything to do with me, but he also didn't see me as a threat. At least at first. His name was Mack Johnson. He was a local guy.

"How are you, John?" he said the first time we met. "You can have at the computers all you want. Any help you need, just ask Tammy."

While Mack himself wasn't very helpful, he wasn't rude. Time spent working at the Commack branch was different again from other offices. I had very little help from the people who worked there, and very little conversation. In Northport, at least, I knew Janice, and she not only clued me into some of the surface activities that were going on but also introduced me to the other staff there, who then accepted me more readily. She brought me more on the inside there, which made Anjali's cold shoulder that much easier to take. At Commack I felt neither necessary nor unnecessary: neither liked nor disliked.

I did have one advantage in Commack, and that was the experience of dealing with Anjali. And so when branch manager Mack Johnson pointed to the computer, I followed his lead and started doing research. I immediately began asking questions about accounts around the office. But again, while the numbers tell a story, it's much more helpful and efficient to gain insight into a client from another banker who already knows them. But since Mack wasn't eager to share his client experiences, I had to try to put the narratives together on my own from the numbers and the occasional note a banker had left on the customer contact in the system. Of course, this was our original contact system, but Jansen had us add the Lotus program, I guess so we could do things twice. As I had mentioned before, the systems didn't interface.

Of course, I had been in touch with my contacts to see if they had any business in Commack and if they knew of anyone who might be interested in meeting with me to talk about their needs and how HSBC might be able to assist. Commack was now another town in which to make myself known—more work to build a new foundation.

*Acct distant
from local branch*

As I got down to my research, I noticed that many of the accounts had a physical address in Manhattan. We were, at best, an hour commute from Manhattan. That would be if it didn't rain or snow and no one was pulled over to the side of the LIE for a ticket or a flat tire. Businesses operating in the city would normally have very little reason to establish accounts outside of Manhattan, or the Burroughs. Typically, the branch an account chose would be in a location that was convenient to their business. If your business was in Commack, you'd likely bank there, or at least establish your account. With HSBC, as with most banks, this procedure is important because this bank will store your live documentation, corporate resolution, and copies of identification. What better place to have your physical documents stored than at the bank nearest your place of business? Of course, this matters less these days, as most big banks and a lot of small ones, too, have imaging systems. A teller in California can see an image of a New York corporation's signature card at their window. Oh, not at HSBC, not with their computer system.

So there were an inordinate number of Manhattan based corporations that banked with Commack. It looked like a trend. As I looked further, I saw that many of the accounts that came out of the city also had accounts in East Northport, and vice versa. At this point, I still wasn't working with the clients as my job entailed. But if the managers weren't going to work with me, then I had to get a clear picture of their operations and learn who I should be contacting to add to my

Lotus Book in the first place. These accounts matched the criteria that would require them to be in my portfolio. I was trying to build an accurate picture of how the branch operated. That's when I noticed that many of these companies had been given loans, which had not been paid and were ultimately charged off. Those loans had originated with Anjali in East Northport and had been finally notarized by Mack in Commack for companies doing business out of New York City.

I was nervous looking at the computer screen. It's amazing how something as benign as a computer screen and an electronic file can make you feel fear. I looked around to see if I was being watched and then put my head back down and further cycled through some of the accounts.

Then on a hunch, I pulled a couple of folders of the borrowing corporations from the unlocked file cabinet. These files should contain copies of applications, financials, and loan documents. I noticed the notary stamp and the signature of Angela Martin on the documents. There were millions of dollars of loans here for companies originating in Manhattan, underwritten by Commack, and notarized by the East Northport business banking specialist—or were they?

I knew what I was looking at right away. I didn't have to ask. The books were crooked. If this had been the old days, I'd have started an immediate investigation and get to the bottom of what had been happening. But these weren't the old days.

Chapter 18

I was in East Northport again for my next scheduled branch visit. It had been about a week since my discoveries at the Commack branch. I was still getting the cold shoulder from Anjali, and I was working on her computer and studying the branch's accounts and finding more fraud and suspicious activity. At one point I began to think that it was my fault that I kept finding the fraud; like when an abused wife blames herself. I thought, "Well, I'm trained to find fraud so I must just be looking for it." But that type of thinking went out the window when I picked two files at random just to see what I came up with: one was connected back to a corporation in Manhattan, which I had already decided was cooking their books, and another was missing some essential information.

That was the moment I knew I had to tell people about my findings. I hadn't come here to make enemies, but this level of corruption was ridiculous and blatant, and I seemed to be at its epicenter. To some extent you can always find fraud in a bank if you look for it. I had already encountered fraud at HSBC that was far more out in the open than I was comfortable with, but what was going on here was a whole new level of corruption that was almost surreal. It was so open and unreported. At times I honestly felt like what I was looking at was a joke, and that Lou would come out from behind a cubicle and say, "Just keeping you on your toes. It was a bit much, I know, but it was fun to watch you squirm." But I would have no such luck. These people really were defrauding the bank.

I got on the phone. I knew that Dan Alton was working out of Commack this week. He worked right under Sanja Malhotra, the district executive VP for Long Island.

"Hey, Dan, it's John Cruz…yeah, I'm fine, but I'm out here in East Northport today and I was in Commack recently and I've been noticing some irregularities in both offices." The irregularities were as crooked as they come, but I didn't want to come right out and say it.

"What kind of irregularities?"

"Well, some of the accounts show no tax returns, or they're not signed. Have you heard of any trouble out in these branches? I mean, I'm in a lot of places during the week, and I keep running into stuff out here."

"No, John, I haven't heard of anything. Everything's supposed to be in order, but if you keep finding stuff let me know, all right? Stay in touch."

After I got off the phone, I went and asked Anjali about the tax returns of one of her clients. I figured we had played around enough and it was time to ask her directly. She danced around at first, and then she got on the phone to contact the client.

"I'll get to the bottom of this," she said. Her phone call was actually a show of confidence in my abilities that I hadn't expected to get from her. She was now calling her client based upon my word. I was actually quite surprised.

They talked small talk for a few minutes, and then she got around to the point. "Yes, we need copies of those returns. Your file is not quite in order. No. Yes, my new senior business relationship manager noticed it. I should introduce you two." Then she organized a trip for the both of us to meet the client.

"I'm sorry I treated you so roughly. I'm glad you brought this to my attention. I've got a meeting scheduled with him and another client in the city two days from now; will you be able to make it?"

A few days later, the two of us were in my car on the way to Manhattan to meet with Mark DeFipo, one of the branch's clients, and also one of the clients whose tax returns were neither completed nor signed. Ostensibly we were going to get the documents from him and allow me the chance to meet with one of her clients for the first time. This was the sort of introduction I'd expected a few weeks ago. I welcomed the opportunity to actually create a relationship with Anjali. I hoped to find out that I was wrong about the "irregularities" I had noticed. I was always happier to find out that I was wrong about someone's corruption then I was to hang it around their necks.

It was midafternoon so traffic was light. We were headed for an office just off the West Side Highway, somewhere near Thirty-fourth Street. We talked for a part of the ride, but whenever I started asking her questions about DeFipo, she clammed up or evaded me. Then she got on her phone. At first she sent texts back and forth and pounded on her little keyboard. Then she started making phone calls. She sounded like she was checking on clients. Then at times she sounded like she was talking to family members. I couldn't tell. I tried not to snoop in her business, but that's always a difficult proposition when the person is openly talking on a phone beside you and you have nowhere else to go.

We arrived at an old yellowish brick building with terracotta ornamentation over the windows and near the roof. Mike DeFipo worked out of a tenth floor office. A portly security guard stood by the bank of elevators and called us in. He got the OK on his phone and then let us onto the elevator. The elevator was old and moved slowly. It had gilt wooden doors. We reached our stop and stepped out. A gaunt secretary greeted us from behind a desk as we came out of the elevator: "Hi, Mike's waiting." She obviously knew Anjali. I followed them through a cluster of low partitions in the large open space and to the back wall of offices. Mike was standing out in front of a wood door that sealed off his small glass walled room, which was really not much more than a glorified closet. His desk was nearly bare except for a couple of files lying out.

"Come in, sit down."

And we followed him into the cramped room and sat in the two chairs opposite the desk. He was an older man, with short-cropped hair and dark brown eyes. His suite was crisp and blue, and he had on a red tie.

"Mike, this is our new senior business relationship manager, John Cruz."

"Hi, John, nice to meet you."

"Likewise."

"Please have a seat."

We began to talk briefly about the education supply company that he ran. "But really all you need are the returns. Sorry about the mistake."

But there was something in the way he talked that unsettled me. He reached out and handed me the set of files off to his right. Then he handed Anjali the set to his left, which was marked especially for her and was noticeably thicker. I wanted to ask, but I think my hesitation must've upset him.

"What?" Mike said.

"There's no reason on earth we should have different, let alone separate files. Not for tax returns."

Anjali looked horrified. But she didn't say a word.

Then Mike got aggressive. I looked back at him when he started shouting. "Listen, you just take those like I give 'em to you. Do whatever she tells you to." Then he stopped and looked over at her. "Anjali, would you handle this?" He stood and backed away from his desk. Then he turned, "I've got somewhere to be," and he walked out.

"What the fuck is the matter with you?" Anjali said to me as we left the office.

"What's the matter with me? What is this? Nothing so far with you is working in the usual way. You can't take me out to meet a client and prove that his tax returns are real, and then have him hand out separate returns. I'm not new, you know. I do this for a living."

I couldn't get a reading on her in that moment. She looked as angry as she looked frightened. But who was she frightened of? In the end, money laundering only occurs under the approval of the bank through which it's laundered. It's not an accident. The person at the bank who agrees to take on the account knows what they are doing, and this is especially true when they endeavor to take on clients without filling in the necessary tax paper work, and business information. This means that, rather than proving who or what their business is, the branch manager simply takes it on without question, which is both against the law and against any bank policy whatsoever.

Anjali then looked at me after a long time of silence.

"We're going back to Northport; this isn't going to work," she said.

We drove back to the branch in silence. Then, as we reached Queens, Anjali took a phone call that shook her up. "Yes. No," she said, "but…but…I'll be there." Then she clicked over and dialed another number. "It's all over," she said. "No, they want me in right now. I have to see security at the Melville branch now."

When she hung up I asked her: "Anjali, what's going on?"

"They say that eighty percent of my loans are in default."

"What, eighty? How could that be? That's fraud."

"Whatever it is, I've got to go. Listen, just don't ask me any more fucking questions."

I shook my head. Now I was like her chauffeur. We drove silently along the LIE. On the way back to East Northport, she made a few more phone calls and sent out a dozen texts. I can only imagine who she was corresponding with. It's possible that she was not just talking to some of her fraudulent clients but up the ladder at HSBC. As I would come to find out from internal security at the bank, this hypothesis is more than likely, as her personal connections with Malhotra the senior VP were well known. Even though her behavior was so strange, I hadn't yet begun to think the worst of her. I had only just met her. In that time she had been terrible to me, and I knew she was embroiled in fraud and that the Mr. DeFipo we had just met with was part of that fraud, but I couldn't have imagined how deep the pool went.

Chapter 19

When I went in to Melville to see Janson the following morning, he wasn't interested in hearing what I had to say. And he didn't care about the separate sets of loan documents the client had given Anjali and me. I was having difficulty understanding how I was supposed to do my job under these circumstances. Now, suddenly, it was my duty to handle new clients at a branch where the manager wouldn't allow me to know who her clients were, and if she did allow me to meet with them, as with DeFipo, I got a different set of documents, which, as illegal and fraudulent behavior goes, is pretty flamboyantly corrupt.

This was hardly my biggest problem. When I asked Janson what was going to happen to Anjali, again I was told, "It's none of your business. I have no idea about any of her loans being in default." But this last statement couldn't possibly be true, or shouldn't have been true, as she worked almost directly beneath him on the food chain. Her activities had a direct impact on his bottom line; he was rated on what business was brought in to the branches. So it was actually his job to know. He was playing stupid or lying or both.

Since leaving HSBC I've had some time to catch up on a little reading. One of my pet topics has been the CIA, and one of the CIA's sayings applies here. They refer to the lies and overlapping confusion of international espionage as "a forest of mirrors," which is exactly where I had found myself. But when I was pulled into it, I didn't realize just how complex the overlapping stories were, or how impossible it would be to get a straight answer or some semblance of the truth; and this, I think, was my error.

What an error: to expect the truth, or to expect that once you've uncovered the truth your coworkers and supervisors will be happy and applaud your honesty! My error, in short, was thinking I could go on with business as usual after I effectively kicked the hornets' nest. But we couldn't go on with business as usual. My discovery of fraud and money laundering was like when one spouse discovers that the other spouse is cheating. After you've learned the truth that your husband is cheating, you never really can go back to the way things used to be. What you've learned has fundamentally changed the tenor of your relationship. Now imagine that the spouse you've just witnessed cheating tells you that you did not see what you saw, and continues not only like things are normal, but also continues cheating.

This was the way it was for me over the following weeks and months. In hindsight, the only way I could have avoided what was coming was to pretend like I hadn't seen the fraud. I even tried to remain in denial about it. The only problem was that it was my job to not only keep and maintain good working relations with clients but to be sure they were running legitimate businesses. Always, always in the back of my mind were the money laundering and fraudulent accounts. How had they gotten the money they needed so badly to hide? I pictured cocaine deals and bundles of cash that then all funneled through a friendly local banker. I thought of kids hooked on crack and families' shattered dreams. It was making me sick. And I knew above all that if those clients were laundering money or committing fraud, it was legally incumbent on me to end their dealings with the bank and to distance myself from them. So, it was almost impossible for me to not find the dirt if the dirt was there to be found. I wasn't about to pretend that I didn't see something like this.

After he told me he knew nothing about what was happening to Anjali, I left Janson's office. I still had to make the rounds of my other branches. I also had to go back to Carle Place and continue to help out over there. I had Thursday afternoon set aside to return to East Northport, yet I hadn't the slightest clue what to expect now that Anjali was in trouble. Part of me thought that everything would come out in the wash. If they discovered that 80 percent of her loans were in default, which is more than just subprime lending but could also be construed as a means of stealing money from the bank through false companies set up expressly for

Their loan
defaults assoc w/ a branch or a client set.

the purpose of receiving loans they'd never pay back, then she was facing serious problems, possibly jail time. The charges against her would only get worse if the auditors or bank security also questioned the validity of the borrowers.

On Wednesday night I prepared for the worst. I had encountered such lying and obfuscation before, but only looking in from outside the maze. Now I was trapped inside.

And so in the morning, I stopped in at the Melville office and gathered up some of my things and then made the trek up to East Northport. When I walked in, I asked Janice where Anjali was.

"She hasn't been in," she said.

"And they haven't told you anything?"

"No, security came, I think it was Steve Esperanza, but I'm not sure. He came and took nineteen or twenty files from her office."

"But they didn't say anything?"

"No," she said, "they just came in here and took the files."

"That doesn't look so good for her."

I called Janson to ask what he wanted me to do. "Just do what you normally do," he replied, seeming irritated that I would even ask. "Don't worry about there being no BM around; that shouldn't hinder you from dealing with the customers." And then he chuckled a bit. "Well, now at least you don't have to worry about her getting jealous of your talking with the clients."

He laughed, but I didn't. What he said wasn't all that funny considering the reason she didn't want me dealing with her clients was because they were corrupt. This was the strangest kabuki dance I had ever been asked to perform in. At least I had access to the customers and to their files, and so I wasn't reliant totally on Anjali for information. And now I didn't have to worry about her looking over my shoulder if I found anything really suspicious.

I signed back onto the computer. I was looking for one name in particular. Janice was watching me over her computer screen. I smirked at her, and she went back to what she was doing. Then I found DeFipo's file. I opened it up and began poring over the different numbers. I hadn't had the chance to thoroughly look through the paper file that he had handed me the other day. I never saw what was in the file he gave to Anjali, but it didn't really matter because I could see what he was doing by just looking at the numbers alone. The numbers would tell the story.

At first I didn't see anything wrong, but then I began to see what was going on. I couldn't tell what or why yet, but the data trail was there. With DeFipo's file it became apparent that he didn't have the income to justify either the loans he had been given or the income streams these accounts showed. The tax returns indicated that the company grossed under twenty thousand dollars that year. The deposit account activity indicated transactions in the millions of dollars weekly. The funds came in the form of electronic transfers that were then withdrawn the same day. The activity sometimes left the account in the red for up to over one million dollars. In no way should an account be allowed to overdraw to that degree. That is tantamount to a loan; it's an extension of credit—for free—which banks don't do. In addition, the overdrafts would have required the approval of someone with lending authority up to the amount of the overdraft. I didn't know who that person was. I couldn't be certain where many of the electronic transfers deposited into the account came from; otherwise I would have followed those also. Many of the transfers came in through PayPal in twenty thousand, forty thousand, and sixty thousand dollar increments. I found this to be another red flag. These multiple increments could very well be an indication that the sender wanted to move a lot of money while staying under the IRS' "radar" that examines transactions over one hundred thousand dollars.

Another oddity was that loans were given to borrowers for the purpose of carrying their receivables. However, these were borrowers whose tax returns and financial statements were prepared on a "cash basis"—that means there were no receivables. It just made me wonder if anyone reviewed these applications before the loans were approved. Lending 101—does the purpose of the loan make sense?

There was an additional fact I picked up on that didn't quite make sense. After some time, I stopped thinking about it and put it aside as an error. But it stuck with me: according to our great computer system, one of the accounts that DeFipo had opened actually closed the day before it was open. However, in that span there was still time to transfer thousands of dollars, again in small sums of twenty, thirty, and sixty thousand dollars. This just left another strange event for me to worry about, just not at this moment, as I had enough on my plate.

I knew I had to report this fraud. It was obvious to me that nothing was as it seemed, and so I printed out the entire file and kept it for myself.

This wasn't an account activity that functioned the way business accounts traditionally work. This was a bloodstream designed to pump money. I had seen it before. It must have been what Anjali was hiding. But in the scheme of things, it wasn't that massive. A little money in and out was common practice. In an industry that at least in part invents money, some people are going to find ways to invent the money for themselves. The thing is, they usually get caught.

Then I saw a PDF at the bottom with the accountant's invoice and the name Ranj Sekar. At least I had another name to follow. If he was the accountant for the business, then he knew what was going on. I called Ranj to see what he could tell me. While the phone rang, I thought to myself, "I know why Janson put me here now; he must have read my file and knew what I was groomed to do." I was beginning to get the picture. Corporations are rumor mills, and if you want something done that goes against the grain, you can't state your intentions too loudly; otherwise the machine will tangle you in its gears. Janson was starting to look to be a lot smarter than he had. He'd suspected the fraud up here. He'd put me here, cooled me off so I didn't cause too many problems or come in like a bull in a china shop, as he knew the card house would come down with just a little pressure on my part. Maybe he wasn't so bad after all.

I let the phone ring. I just wanted to poke around and see where the rabbit hole went. Besides, it was actually my job to do the due diligence and know if these businesses were legitimate or not. There is a term of law in banking called "willful blindness." If you are aware of money-laundering activity, or even suspect money-laundering activity, you are responsible to report it. If you don't, you are considered as guilty as the perpetrator because you acted in "willful blindness." And this goes one step further: if you do report it and nothing is done about it and you know that nothing has been done about it, you must go over the heads of whomever you first reported and report it again. If you don't you are still as guilty as the perpetrator.

In the eighties there was a similar term in politics called "plausible deniability." It's the same concept, only in banking you can be held personally liable for being willfully blind. In politics you're just clever. But I wasn't going to be willfully blind. Not ever.

The rabbit hole would take me only so far today. The phone rang and rang, but no one answered, and there was no answering service. Mr. Ranj Sekar, the accountant for DeFipo, was beginning to look like another phantom.

Chapter 20

"Morning." I had been waiting for Janson to arrive. It was Friday. I was happy to hand in my report on fraud. I thought he would be pleased with me.

"Why aren't you at Northport meeting with the clients there?"

"I found fraud there with the client DeFipo that Anjali had me meet the other day, the one with the duplicate, falsified tax returns—but there's more to it than that. I went back to the computers after I saw the double returns and looked into his deposit account activity. He's been funneling more money in a week through his accounts than his company grosses in a year, and his books are—"

"I don't want to fuckin' hear about it."

I couldn't believe it. "What? What did you send me there for then?"

"You're supposed to be handling clients and getting new ones. No one told you to go investigate people's accounts like you're some fucking detective."

"Excuse me. I can't handle my clients if the books are cooked."

"You know you're crazy, John? Everything is fuckin' crooked to you."

"I've found fraud and possible money laundering out of HSBC branches, and I don't want anything to do with it over there. It's company policy to pull me out of there and run an investigation."

"Well, you're not going back to Carle Place, so you can forget about it. Just get out of my office and go work on your client portfolio. I don't have time for this shit."

He was obviously on another planet. Either that or we spoke in different languages, and after having worked for this corporation I think this last is true. He spoke the English of HSBC, an international bank that could make up whatever it wanted as long as it had money to pay, while I still spoke American, and I didn't realize I could make things up as I pleased as long as they fit with the company line. The company was the truth, and the truth was the company.

I walked out. I didn't know what to do. I had never dealt with anyone like Janson before. I couldn't tell if he was just an asshole or if he was trying to avoid a scandal or if he was just totally incompetent. Either way, my theory that he had sent me there because I was such an honest and upright guy with solid experience in detecting fraud was out the window. What the hell had I been thinking? He didn't care about the fraud. As far as I could tell, he didn't care about anything if he didn't think of it first. I'm sure if it had dawned on him that there was fraud in that deposit account, and he had sent me to uncover it, he would have been all over this. But since he didn't and the fraud came from outside of his game plan, he was upset and didn't want to hear anything about it. Either that, or he didn't want to lose one-third of this branch's production and have to turn in a bad earnings report in a year when things were already looking bad and layoffs and branch closings were imminent. In this case it was my job just to keep my fucking mouth shut, as I am sure he would have put it.

The only thing I could do now was to get back to work and continue to develop my relationship with the legitimate clients from the branches I was working. Once again, I was called to Carle Place to help Cicero with some of my old clients. A few of them had been complaining to me privately. They were not happy with him and felt he was neglectful. I took care of Cicero's needs and got back on the road to East Northport. I was looking forward to a business meeting with one of my legitimate clients there. Actually doing my job was a refreshing change. I signed back on to my computer to make some phone calls with the purpose of setting some appointments with clients. Strangely, I felt some sort of anguish, as though I was doing something wrong by looking into my clients' accounts. I had to remind myself that this was my job. I was expected to not see what I saw and not to talk about it.

I waved hello to Janice as I entered, thinking it was funny how employees will keep coming to work even when everything is up in the air. Janice knew the bank was in chaos. They had no branch manager, and something big was going on. But she came to work and did her job. When I went into the back office, she came in behind me. "You want coffee, John?"

"Yeah, I could take a coffee."

After coffee and some chitchat, I signed back onto the system and searched for the largest accounts to review. There I noticed accounts under the name Goldfarb. From what I could tell so far, he had multiple accounts through a shipping company, Shipping Express, that was moving millions of dollars from Manhattan; it was such a large account that I had to know more about it. I thought they might be a good candidate for our Cash Management Program. I ran a Social Security search to be sure I had an accurate listing of all his entities and deposit and loan accounts. This was standard procedure, of course. If I was going to meet with a client and make suggestions as to what he might need, I had better know what he had with us already.

I typed in his number, and the result came back that there was a match to that SS number with 5,247 accounts. "Oh my God," I thought.

I pulled back from my computer and shook my head. "Five thousand accounts," I thought, "this is going to be fun." The first thing I did was print the computer screen listing his accounts. It took a little while. Getting the hard copy was a "must do" that Lou had taught me to be certain that what you found remained what you found. Computer systems in banks have a way of changing overnight, or even while you look at them.

To this extent, HSBC was not only *not* an exception to the rule; it was at the cutting edge of flipping numbers in the system even despite the fact of its antiquated, overlapping programs.

A couple of paper jams and a toner change later, I started to review the printouts. As far as I could tell, there were accounts at multiple branches throughout Manhattan, Long Island, and the United States. I didn't need to have another suspicious client. However, opening multiple accounts at multiple branches is a sign of fraud and is not a standard bank practice. Let's not forget to mention the five thousand some odd accounts and thousands of credit cards or lines of credit. It was more than suspicious.

Making matters worse, our dinosaur of a computer system did not differentiate some lines of credit from some credit cards. Our product development people only added to the confusion. Clients could have a line of credit in a place that was attached to their checking account to cover overdrafts; it also worked as a credit card and was assigned a credit card number. If clients had a credit card and a checking account, they could elect to have the accounts affiliated to cover overdrafts. Without going too far into bank minutia, the point is that I had uncovered under Goldfarb's SSN tons of credit whether in the form of a line of credit or a credit card. Either way, it was fraud.

Looking deeper, I found that there were other fraudulent accounts associated with his Social Security number. My job was to follow my client's money and determine how it was allowed to flow through the bank. I discovered that the Social Security number Goldfarb used was reported as stolen. There in plain sight in plain English was a warning on his loan request that the SSN was reported stolen. Needless to say, I was floored.

I looked even deeper, or I should say farther outside the US, and discovered that accounts were being opened using the names and identities of unsuspecting people in South America and Asia. I found billions of dollars that was likely laundered money. Goldfarb himself had over $855 million going through his accounts, which were affiliated with the thousands of accounts that shared the stolen SSN around the world. My heart raced and my head spun. My continuing search came to a sudden dead end as I was locked out of the international segment of the system without warning.

That was just a minor setback. There was still plenty of research I could do. I continued looking inside the US and found accounts opened on July 10 and closed the day prior. This didn't make any sense at all. I remembered catching it before. Reviewing the account, I found millions of dollars that were transferred through the accounts just like these. Based on what I figured out from our customer information system, the date switch was being done to hide fraudulent transactions done in the name of Mr. & Mrs. John Q. Public, and Sr. & Sra. Juan Q. Publico, and M. & Mme. Jean Q. Publique.

The closed accounts would be purged from the system as of the closing date, causing the transactions to disappear like ledgers written in disappearing ink. This, of course, would only work on a crappy computer

Acct open after close to purge transactions

system…or was the system designed to allow the money laundering? These were not interest-bearing accounts either, so the account holders were never sent interest-earning statements. The bank never had to report them to anyone; there was no interest to report to the IRS. These were sub accounts used to launder money using the public's names. Those folks might never know the accounts existed. Threading this information together, I had a better understanding of how the fraud was being perpetrated. The bank was knowingly facilitating the laundering of money using the identity of innocent people. And to top it all off a portion of the funds were put to the side to pay any fines should they get caught.

One of the three layers of a typical money-laundering scenario is to layer multiple accounts. This was layering on a grand scale, and all the accounts were taking in PayPal money at twenty-, forty-, and sixty-thousand-dollar clips to keep under the one-hundred-thousand-dollar reporting level, and then turning that money back over the same day; just as with DeFipo but on a larger scale. The money went in and out, in and out. And some of the accounts had been granted loans, which had been submitted by Anjali but rejected by the underwriter. The underwriter's job is to review the application and the loan's purpose and perform an analysis on the applicant's financials, which includes understanding the nature of the business, among many other analytical tasks. The point of all of this is to determine the level of risk that the bank would take on by approving the loan.

- How long is the account open for ⇒ did it ever generate a statement?

After the underwriter had rejected the loans, they were then notarized by Mack Johnson in Commack. I had seen this pattern before. Then I noticed another little coincidence: the accountant was the same as from the DeFipo file. It was Ranj Sekar again.

But who would underwrite these garbage loans to fraudulent companies whose numbers were so out of whack that even the most novice banker or auditor would catch this at first glance? I looked through and found that on two of the loans the initial underwriter had not signed off. In fact, this person John Marks had turned down the application, which had then been signed by Sanja Malhotra, the district executive and senior executive vice president—not a lender. He had credit authority based on his position and could override an underwriter's decision. Marks must have loved that.

But what was Sanja Malhotra, SVP of Long Island, doing approving these loans? How did Anjali get his authorization and approval on a deal where the fraud was so obvious? I couldn't have wanted any less to do with this right now. This was *not* my job anymore. Of course, I was supposed to discover fraud in a branch if it was going on, but my job was to retain business clients and bring in new ones, not to acquire new territory and spend all of my time sorting out fraud there. And this had every indication of money laundering now. When you are seeing millions of dollars from the alleged sale of school supplies moving through an account per week, but you don't show that you gross that much in a year, something is seriously wrong. Or in the case of this Goldfarb character, $855 million in fraud. The full amount wasn't apparent right away, but what was apparent was that it was another case of fraud. The problem now was that it no longer appeared to involve just a couple of branch managers. This was on the regional level.

I had never seen fraud on this scale before. This was now a regional head in a major international bank responsible for signing off on bad loans to an account holder with some five thousand accounts and no way to write down all the cash funneling through them, or at least not based on any of the numbers he was supposed to be grossing on his tax returns. Furthermore, and again, the tax returns were not signed, and several lines had been left blank.

Here was a small shipping company that did not own a single truck moving enough money through our bank to make an offer to buy FedEx. I wanted to call Lou and tell him about just how big this was, but I was too worried about it to call and ask advice. In a sense, I didn't want Lou to have the burden of knowing.

I made up my mind to have a meeting with Malhotra. He had underwritten the loans. I should at least let him know. And besides, I had already gone to both Janson and Dan Alton. I left a message with Mr. Sanja Malhotra's secretary and explained how I had discovered some very troubling irregularities originating out of Commack and East Northport. She told me that he would call back as soon as he had a free moment. I wasn't going to hold my breath, but I was optimistic that he'd at least call back.

Chapter 21

The next pattern I noticed, not simply in Yael Goldfarb's file, but all over, was that several of the businesses I was looking over all had the same address. I only noticed it because Thirty-fourth and Broadway was easy to remember, and once I picked it out a few times, I started looking for it then on purpose. By eleven o'clock I had a list of seven businesses all with the same address.

At this point, I was certain I was holding the locations of more fraudulent companies that were all most likely related. On the other hand, it's not unheard of to pick up multiple accounts at the same address. If you have business in one building that holds multiple tenants, any good salesperson will work to acquire the business of any number of other companies in the same location. When I actually had the luxury of pre-call planning, I'd pick a prestigious building and do a reverse directories search by address to get a list of occupants. Next, I would check the Department of State or County for ownership information—all free on the

Internet. Then, I would run a Google search on the business and owners. After that, I'd use a research program we had at the bank to check out that particular industry. Therefore, what looked like a casual cold call was in reality an educated, well-planned visit designed to bring in business.

Therefore, just because these other businesses shared the address with Goldfarb didn't necessarily mean they were fake. However, they needed to be looked into. Actually, whoever set up the accounts might have intentionally nested Goldfarb in among this group of real businesses in a thriving building in order to shield him. There is something known as "mailbox" addresses. An office is set up in an area known for successful businesses. The office itself is simply a bunch of mailboxes that collect and forward the business mail to wherever. Any number of answers was possible. I wouldn't know if I didn't head to Manhattan and check it out.

It took about an hour and a half to get there. It was an old building a few blocks from Macy's Herald Square. I walked into the lobby of the building and went up to the directory that was posted on the wall opposite the door. It was the standard black plastic type with white letters pressed into the surface, housed behind a Plexiglas and aluminum case with a lock. I looked over the list and noticed something interesting. None of the businesses I was looking for operated here.

When I saw that, I went to the security desk and asked for the building manager, who happened to be in. I showed him the list of businesses.

"Yes, HSBC," I said. "I just picked up these accounts, and I'm out to meet the clients for the first time. Here's the address, but I don't see them listed."

He went back to his files. "They've never been here."

But it wasn't really a mystery. I hadn't expected that all of them would end up being fake, but it wasn't really a surprise. The manager was a little frightened. I think he thought maybe I would accuse him or at least implicate him in something. But I had a pretty good idea that he wasn't Goldfarb, and he sure as hell had never met Anjali.

I went back out to my car and phoned the East Northport office, asking for Janice. I knew that she probably had nothing to do with what had been going on in the office.

"What are you finding out there?" she asked dubiously.

"I found that all seven of those businesses don't exist, nor have they ever existed at this address. That's what I've found."

"That was Goldfarb, right?" she asked.

"Yeah, him and a few others."

"I have a number on him here if you want it."

"There's a number?" I was shocked.

"You want it?"

"Of course."

I couldn't believe there was a phone number on this guy. I had started to think he was a fabrication.

She gave me the number. It was a 516, Long Island number. I dialed and he answered. Go figure.

"May I speak with Yael Goldfarb?"

"Speaking."

"Mr. Goldfarb, hello, my name is John Cruz. I'm the new senior business relationship manager for the East Northport branch of HSBC. I've been stopping by some of the new accounts I've acquired in Manhattan today. I'm outside your Thirty-fourth Street address, and I can't seem to find you."

"I'll be there in fifteen minutes," he said. Then he hung up the phone.

I was beside myself with shock. Was this guy really going to show up? I didn't expect him to be real, let alone have a live phone number that someone could actually reach him on. So I had no idea whether he would show up here or not. But exactly fifteen minutes later, he called me back.

"Yeah, sorry about that," he said. "I just got off the phone with your office, it's all taken care of."

"OK, who did you talk with at the office?"

"Anjali, it's all taken care of."

Now I was really sick to my stomach. "I'd like to have the opportunity to meet with you to get to know you personally. And I have some questions I need to ask you about the accounts you have specifically."

"Sorry, you're going to have to speak to Anjali on that."

"Then do you know where I can reach her?"

He answered me by ending the call again.

Chapter 22

On my drive back to Melville, I was running through the recent events as fast as I could, trying to get some sense of what had happened. I knew there was fraud. I had the evidence on a large scale that involved at least one branch manager and an accountant who had some affiliation with the bank. On top of that, the district executive and SVP were involved with the loan that had been issued and then charged off.

Like it or not, it appeared to be fate that fraud would be a continuing theme in my existence here with HSBC. I didn't know how to handle it. I knew what I was supposed to do by law and by corporate procedure and policy. But I was being stopped from handling it the right way. So, what I really didn't know was how to handle the being warned not to handle it. Legally the bank had to turn fraud over to the authorities. HSBC policy dictated that I report my findings to my supervisor, but since Janson had been reluctant to hear anything about fraud, I would have to go over his head.

I bypassed the Melville branch and went right to Northport. I wanted to speak with Janice for a few minutes, and I wanted another look at the computer system. When I walked into her office, she smiled. "You look like you had a nice time of it."

"I got Goldfarb on the phone."

"God, I never thought he'd answer."

"He said he would show up to the building in fifteen minutes. But he didn't. He called and said that he had talked with Anjali and it was all taken care of."

"That what was taken care of? She's not even here anymore."

"I don't know, he hung up. That was it."

"What are you going to do?" she asked.

"I don't know yet."

"You should talk to Angela about this. She found something similar. Remember she had her notary stamp duplicated?"

"Yeah I remember, but how does that help me now? What am I going to do with all this fraud I'm finding? I can't just pretend it's not there."

"Report it," she said.

"Why the hell won't they move me? Janson sure as hell won't do anything about it. Come Monday he won't even want to know what I found."

"Why don't you go up the ladder? Take it to Malhotra, and if he won't listen to you then take it to Art Jacobs. The fraud is there; you're either going to pretend you don't see it and go on with business as usual, in which case you're going to have to at least in part maintain business with the clients, or you're going to have to turn them in and turn over everything you find."

I already knew what I had to do, but it was good to hear it from someone else. It was a relief to get some sort of encouragement.

"I put a call into to Sanja already when I found he underwrote some of the loans."

She raised her eyebrows at me. "I wouldn't have guessed," she said.

"Yeah, well, it's there in black and white."

"You should be in charge of security."

"Then they wouldn't have a business."

But then she suddenly stopped smiling and looked at her computer screen. "Oh my God," she said.

"What is it?"

A smirk covered her face as she started to read from her screen: "It's an e-mail from corporate about Anjali; they say she's resigned from the bank effective immediately to pursue her passion of interior design. She has maintained her interest in this vocation for many years and has now just gotten the opportunity to follow it, and so she is taking that opportunity. Blah, blah, blah."

"What a lie." It could be nothing other than a lie. One of your employees is embroiled in massive fraud over multiple accounts, implicating an SVP, and she suddenly disappears to pursue her "passion." One thing was for sure: either they had removed her or she'd removed herself, but HSBC needed this episode of its history to stay buried. The only problem was that I was left with the mess, and I didn't want to just eat it. There was a paper trail that went far beyond her to the upper levels of senior management; I already could see that much. And besides, I wouldn't just remain quiet, not even for the purpose of covering my own ass. Most important-ly, I wanted to avoid being the one who got whacked by corporate in their little whack-a-mole game. Would they dare try to put this on me? I saw how it could play out: I am assigned a portfolio of clients from both the East Northport and Commack branches. I uncover fraudulent activity and report it to my boss who all but tells me to look the other way. I do. After that, my name stays on the accounts because it was put into my port-folio, and the next thing I know the fraud is mine. Like "hot potato." When the music stops, I'm left standing there with a great big burning hot potato in my hand.

This was not going to happen. Lou had taught me well. He had instilled in me the importance of al-ways doing the right thing and of being able to prove that I did the right thing to back it up, aka cover your own ass. Typically, when anyone was accused of par-ticipating in fraudulent activity, they tried to implicate the one who uncovered it. And if you weren't careful, you would suddenly become the worst employee the world has ever known. If they could find anything on you, you were done, and if you turned a blind eye to it at any time then you were just as guilty when you did suddenly come forward.

I had only one choice, and that was to make it known what I had discovered. If Janson was not going to listen to me then I would have to climb the ladder. Sanja Malhotra, the senior vice president of all Long

Island branches, wasn't returning my calls. So I decided to go after Art Jacobs, the executive regional president of Metro New York. It was actually my duty to approach Jacobs now, as I was certain Malhotra was involved. I telephoned his office and asked for him by name, as if he were my good friend from way back. Jean, the secretary, hesitated a moment before asking me my name and the purpose of my call.

She put me on hold for a few minutes and returned to say that Jacobs would meet with me in three weeks. I wasn't happy about the wait time, but I would suffer it. In the meantime, I tried my best not to even go into the East Northport branch. I figured I had about a 90 percent chance of finding fraud there, and I didn't even want to see it or touch it. Every new case that I found was another weight around my neck, and every time I discovered fraud and turned it in, it meant less money that the bank was seeing. My portfolio was being eroded due to no fault of my own. There was no offer made to me to adjust my numbers either. Deposit and loan balances just evaporated. So much of my time had been exhausted in researching my "new clients." I was spinning my wheels at East Northport. I needed to get some real productive work done with some normal, hardworking business clients.

Chapter 23

A few days later, I was out in Suffolk County performing a site visit on a company called S&S that had accounts out of East Northport. I pulled up to the address that was listed in the paperwork and found the company didn't even exist. I'd had a feeling they were fake. There was something about it that felt strange. I had only come out here because I was already making rounds for some of my other branches, and I was literally driving by the place so I stopped in. By this point, when I saw the empty building, I wasn't shocked. I was just going to make a note of it on the file and possibly send Janson a halfhearted e-mail, just so I was on record having discovered it. But then I looked back at my laptop to the files on S&S. They had just been issued a loan, and they didn't even exist. But as I looked more closely at the file on my computer screen I noticed something peculiar in their loan docs. I was the notary for the signers of the loan. It was an Anjali deal that had been underwritten in the traditional way, but it was notarized with my stamp right beside my signature. She had duplicated the stamp and forged my signature.

I got on the phone with Janson. He kept me waiting on hold. When he finally came on the line, he said, "You gotta be quick, John, I don't have that much time."

"This will be quick. I just noticed a loan issued two weeks ago, after Anjali disappeared to pursue her passion, signed by her and notarized by me."

"John, these loans are none of your business; you shouldn't waste your time speculating about when Anjali was here to sign a loan or not…"

I cut him off: "It's my business when I didn't notarize the loan."

"Well what the fuck does that mean?"

"It means she got my stamp, or had a hard copy of it made."

"She has your stamp? You're fuckin' crazy."

"I'm going to the police on this. I think my stamp has been duplicated." He was quiet now, and I wondered if he'd hung up. "Are you still there, Mitch?"

"Well, if you think your notary stamp has been tampered with in any way, John, then it's incumbent upon you to notify the police; only remember you're not allowed to discuss anything that goes on inside the bank. Do you understand that? It is against policy."

"I understand that."

We finished, and I headed to the Suffolk County Police Department, Fourth Precinct. I didn't like being there. I didn't like the cold feeling it gave me. The thought crossed my mind that I could be suspected of committing fraud. This was a nightmare.

I began telling the desk officer what had happened. He was helpful and very nice, even if his voice was difficult to hear over the din in the precinct. I completed a report at his request and returned it to him. He gave me a copy of the complaint. I took the claim ticket and went home. Another day at the office.

Two weeks passed. All the while I kept finding new fraud. Sometimes I would hand it in in person to Janson; other times I'd just e-mail it to him. And up at East Northport, we still had no BM.

The Commack branch was no better. I didn't even want touch my clients up there, the fraud was so bad. And Janson was breathing down my neck, complaining that my job performance was lacking. Every time I reported an incidence of fraud, I could count on a phone call telling me to pick up the pace. He would give me the standard corporate speech about how he knew I could do it—"I know you're up to it, John"—like he was reading handouts from his last motivational training seminar. The only problem with his speeches was that he was just wallpapering over the hole. And now that I think of it, maybe that's what those speeches are designed for. Either way, what I got from him was all stick and no carrot. He would not acknowledge that what I had found was fraud. He would not hear of it. He didn't want to know how much of my time and energy was being sucked out of me due to corporate thieves working with money-laundering clients. He didn't know how much I yearned just to do my job, the job I really did love. And I am sure beyond a shadow of a doubt that he was documenting his side of every pep talk phone call he made to me. He was preparing my human resources file for my exit; he couldn't get me on board in spite of all his hard work and encouragement.

It was sometime in early July, just before I met with Art Jacobs. I stopped into Janson's office to drop off some files that were obviously fraudulent. "Get the fuck out of my office, John. Your job is not to find fraud. It's to make accounts, you understand?"

It was at that moment that I knew for certain he was going to get rid of me in whatever way he could. I had been uncovering fraud for about a month, and since Janson had decided it didn't exist, soon I wouldn't exist in his world either. I knew I had gone too far with him and that it was over for me. It didn't matter if I started playing ball with him now; he was going to root me out.

I had waited intently for my meeting with Art Jacobs in hopes that he would finally give me a fair hearing. He was high enough up the ladder that he was outside of Janson's reach, and even Malhotra's.

"John, nice to finally meet with you," he had greeted me. "Now what's this I hear about your finding fraud?"

I had brought files with me, and I had many of the printouts that I had taken off the customer information system.

"I wouldn't worry about this too much, John. Yes, it seems like there is some nonstandard behavior here, but it's nothing to concern yourself with. The employee whose name is on these accounts is no longer employed with HSBC. So there's no need to press this any further."

"Any further? But what about those loans signed by Sanja on a cash basis, when the underwriter wouldn't touch them?"

"It seems a standard practice that when the risk is elevated, the normal underwriter will pass it off to the vice president or someone like that."

"But the loans are now charge-offs. They're losses."

"Is there something you want to accuse Mr. Malhotra of? Or are you just making accusations without any substantiation?"

"Excuse me, but I have files upon files of substantiation."

"You'll do well to forget about this."

And that was that. I took my files with me. No one was going to listen, and now Janson was calling on the phone. I answered. He wanted to know why, according to Lotus Notes, I hadn't made the requisite number of phone calls last month.

"Well, I've been spending so much of my time trying to decipher which clients are fraudulent or not. I don't want to make any more calls to businesses that don't exist."

"It says here you only made twelve calls to new clients."

"Well, I made at least thirty."

"Then why isn't it written down? And you do not have ten kept appointments for this week."

"Of course I do."

"Then why isn't it written in your Lotus Notes calendar? You've really got to step it up, John. I'll help you, but you have to allow me to. OK, we can work together. I believe in your ability."

Whenever he talked to me now it was in this same vein. I knew he was going through the formalities to get rid of me.

Chapter 24

A day or so after Janson scolded me for my Lotus Notes not being up-to-date, I got a call from one of Anjali's old clients. He must have tried to reach me at the branch and was given my cell number by one of the staff in the East Northport office. He called me while I was having lunch: chicken, lettuce, and tomato on whole wheat. As a rule, I brown bagged a healthy lunch nearly every day. I was on the way to East Northport and stopped in the parking lot of a small marina on the harbor to feed my belly and my soul. I was looking for just a couple of minutes of peace and enjoying the breeze.

The client wanted to discuss the possibility of acquiring another loan for his company.

"OK, great. Just let me get back to the office. I'm in the car right now, but as soon as I have access to the computers again I'll call you." I watched a seagull swoop down to grab the piece of bread that I tossed out the window.

Janice greeted me as I walked in, and I sat at her desk with her to catch up. We talked. She was always a good source for reliable information. Today she had something else to tell me; we had a visitor.

"You remember Angela Martin?"

I remembered her, all right.

"The banking specialist. She thought she uncovered fraud a few months ago. Her name's on some of the paperwork you were finding. Anjali was using her. That's her right there."

I approached the desk where Angela was seated and introduced myself. We exchanged pleasantries for a minute. Angela was a petite young woman, professional, who was at the beginning of her banking career. The conversation quickly moved to business. She scowled when I brought up some of the loans I had seen with her name on them.

"I really can't talk about this now. I'm not supposed to." She seemed apprehensive.

I didn't want to frighten her, and I tried to calm her by changing the subject. I asked how business was in Babylon and Bay Shore where she had been transferred after East Northport. She actually rose from her chair, turned, and walked into the small employee kitchenette. I wasn't going to follow her. I looked back at Janice; she let out a stifled laugh and shook her head. She had witnessed the entire exchange between Angela and me. I shook my head back and walked over to the files to pull the information on the client I had spoken with earlier.

His file revealed another obvious sham. He wasn't as overt as Goldfarb, but it looked like he'd be up there on the top fifty fraudsters. He had multiple accounts in several branches, and his income statement did not corresponded with the huge amounts of money that flowed through the account. Based on what he showed in receivables (none) and profits (none), he didn't show that the company had the ability to repay the existing loan. I could not justify lending him more.

"I'm sorry, but based on your financials from the last year end you won't qualify for any additional borrowings."

"What the fuck do you mean you can't give me a loan?"

I didn't like when clients yelled at me, especially when they were crooked.

"Listen, you don't show enough income,"

"Fuck income. Where's Anjali? Put that bitch on the phone."

"She doesn't work here anymore."

"You either do what I tell you or I'll put a bullet in your head. You fucking hear me?"

I hung up the phone. I was shaking a little with anger. I pulled away from the desk. Janice looked at me with the phone receiver to her ear. She held her hands up to signal a question. As I walked over to her, she put the phone down.

"One of Anjali's clients said he was going to put a bullet in my head if I didn't issue him a loan."

I called Janson.

"You know, John, if you're going to make a charge like that you had better have proof."

I was shaking again when I hung up the phone. It was over for me, and I knew it. I had gone as high up the ladder as I could get, but I had hardly gotten my complaints on the record. Now Janson was talking to me as if I were hysterical; either that or he sounded like an official document. I knew how they were going to play it now. He didn't care about the fraud because he didn't want to hurt his bottom line. That was the bottom line. It was easier to railroad me than it was to take appropriate steps and admit what had happened. It was easier to keep it quiet and play it out over the course of a year as they slowly buried these events in the past. It didn't happen, it never happened, and I was just an employee who couldn't handle his work load. They would phase me out.

I also knew that simply as a matter of survival now, I needed to build a case against HSBC that was strong enough to insulate me from their attacks, and eventually bring it to the attention of the police.

Chapter 25

Soon after, I got my first written warning. I knew it was coming. The language Janson had used on the phone when he reprimanded me was too much like the language of a written warning to be a coincidence. The irony that stuck out in my mind about getting that first written warning was how just a few months back I had been written up for excellence. I had crossed every *t* and dotted every *i*. I had never failed at any of the jobs I ever had, going all the way back to the farm, but now they said I was failing. And I felt like I was failing. It's one thing to talk about corruption at work, and it's another to be surrounded by it. It affected my day-to-day life. I dreaded going into the Northport branch because I knew I would only step in more shit—either a bad loan or a bad deposit. And I knew it wouldn't matter to anyone but me. The money would continue to pump through the accounts in total disregard for the laws.

I would source new and legitimate clients, and work with the legitimate, established clients, but just the thought of so many accounts that were literally criminal started to wear me down—especially when I was getting calls from people who were threatening my life. Things like that can tend to wreck your day, or life. I wanted to do more about it.

Then one day I was talking with Janice in Northport. She was asking me about where I had gotten with the fraudulent accounts.

"Nowhere," I said. "Janson just wants to pretend they didn't even happen. I am simply to get to work and 'step it up.'"

"But what are you doing?"

"Janson has basically cut me off. If I even breathe a word about fraud, he goes insane. He gave me a written warning for below-standard job performance."

"You've got to get it on record."

"I went up the ladder to Jacobs, and he told me to put my head back in the sand. It's just a matter of time now. It's either me or them, and it won't be them."

But then she said something that absolutely made my month.

"You know that most of the executives are going on vacation at around the same time?"

"Yeah, so?"

"Well there's enough overlap that Malhotra, Janson, and Jacobs will all be out on Monday, which will put Duggan in charge."

"Are you kidding me?" I couldn't believe it, but it was true. These guys couldn't have gone on vacation at a better time. I knew James cared; I knew he would help. Saturday and Sunday could not go quickly enough for me. On Monday I walked into James's office bright and early. "This can't be good," he said when he saw me.

"No, it's not. I uncovered a tremendous amount of fraudulent activities in several branches. Most if it had Anjali's name on it. But there were plenty of others for sure." I proceeded to show him the different printouts of deposits and loan accounts and showed him how the activity was being carried out. He had access to the computer system at a much higher level of clearance than I did. He also had access to even more of the information I was blind to, like where different transactions came from and what borders they crossed. This was stuff that prosecutors could hardly get even when they had an iron-clad case. Once he saw the duplication of accounts under the same SS numbers, on top of the loans with no source of repayment being declined then decisions reversed, and the withdrawal of same day deposits and loan proceeds, he knew he was looking at fraud.

"We have to go to security with this." He picked up the phone and dialed the head of security, Steve Esperanza.

"Steve, yeah, Duggan, I've got an SBRM here who's found what looks like a whole pile of fraud and laundering coming out of several branches. Yeah, yeah. He's here."

And then I waited for the head of security for the area to come over to meet with me. It's funny I hadn't gone to him before, but I was following protocol. His office was in Manhattan, and it was usually the branch managers who contacted him for their employees when they thought the situation warranted it. Apparently nothing I found so far had warranted Janson's calling security.

But waiting for Steve Esperanza, I decided I should protect myself. I had begun to realize that the corporation protects the corporation, and its many parts will all turn against the individual who steps out of line. And I was stepping out of line. The corporation had to protect itself against me. I had to protect myself from them. I was conflicted. Should I continue to work for this corporation hoping someone would listen to me? Was I righteous or did I just want to win? But I wasn't winning here; no one was.

In my career I've noticed a tendency of some bankers that I've always sworn not to have. It's based on the idea that when someone is on the outside looking in, they often respect the process, whatever process that is. In banking, when you set up a checking account and a line of credit, there is a process to follow, a process that seems not only natural but mandated from on high, and the officers that issue the account share in that mandate. But there are those who are a part of the process who come to scorn the process, and this is what I can't stand. They think the system is a sham, and they think it's a sham because they administer it. This is one of the things Lou taught me: the contempt you feel for the system when you've learned how it works and have come to help administer it is based on the low opinion of yourself. Because if a person with such low standards can come to administer in a system, then the whole system must be a sham. "But if you

182

believe you are measured by the standard, then you will respect the standard," Lou said.

And I respected the standard. I thought it kept me safe. It was part of my identity. I knew that the more people who believed their attitude and behavior didn't matter would only help to increase the number of people whose attitudes and behavior were out of control. Apply this to a bank, and you have one bloated money-laundering system of corruption that only wears the paint of legitimacy. If the people at the top levels think in this way, they turn their company into a feed trough for corruption, while the people at the bottom are held to two standards. The first is that they themselves must follow the rules. The next is that no matter what they see, they must keep their mouths shut.

While working at the credit union I had discovered many instances of fraud, but I had never been expected to become part of that fraud. Nor was what I uncovered then on this scale. The worst case of fraud I had ever found at the credit union was about 1.4 million over the course of a year. At HSBC it was about triple that number a week, sometimes more.

So if I couldn't get away from the fraud and I couldn't just turn away from it, then what was I to do? I was reluctant to turn the bank into the authorities because I was so accustomed to following protocol and having that protocol work. I had trouble fathoming the situation when the system was rigged to hide corruption. At the Long Island Federal Credit Union, when I'd found fraud, I'd moved it through the appropriate channels. The system didn't try to destroy me.

I stepped out to grab a quick lunch and to buy a tape recorder. In the car, I stuffed it into my pocket and turned it on. Then I talked for a few seconds and played it back. The quality was poor, but I figured it would do. I was unprepared to accept fraud, but neither would I be pushed around, and there was no telling whose side this head of security was on; even in thinking back, I'm still not sure.

Steve Esperanza was a short, stocky man with dark hair and glasses that he only wore to look at the computer screen with. I greeted him outside the office James had set aside for us. Esperanza wasted no time getting to the point.

"What do you have for me?"

Instead of going into the computer system, which I'm sure he thought I was going to do, I pulled out the printouts and handed them to him, along with some of the physical files we had at East Northport. Then I pulled my chair close to his desk and showed him the multiple accounts under Goldfarb that Anjali had helped to create, and the accounts under DeFipo along with the loans. I pointed out how the monies came in through PayPal in twenty-, thirty-, forty-, and sixty-thousand-dollar denominations and then were withdrawn same day, and how different accounts were allowed to go into the red for days at a time for multiple hundreds of thousands of dollars—and these were just a few of the accounts.

"I only just got there, and I found all this stuff. I went to my section leader, but he told me I was crazy."

"He said that?"

"Yeah, he said that all right."

"Who else did you go to?" he asked me.

"I went to Jacobs, too," I said.

"Well, you should have come to me sooner."

"I didn't know that I could or how it worked. I was following protocol."

"I know all about the protocol. Here's my number; call me whenever you see this stuff again."

Then Esperanza looked over the files I had brought him. Most of the fraudulent behavior was so easily spotted and so large that it was really striking, and he was reading the files like they were some suspense thriller.

"I can't believe you found all this stuff. I knew there was fraud coming out of there, but I never had any idea how much there really was. This is ridiculous, God, you should work for me."

I laughed a little when he said that. "Yeah, that's not the first time I heard that."

"But I can't do anything about this. My job is to report the fraud up the ladder to the same people you've already spoken to. It's against their rules for me to go outside the company, which means I can't involve the police if I want to keep my job."

This was the same position I felt I was in. I said to him, "Well, what can we do? They're making me eat this stuff. I have to pretend like it's not there. I can't keep going on like this with some of these accounts still active."

"I know. And I can't even report everything," he said.

"What do you mean?

"I mean that I'm only allowed to report 10 percent of what I find. That's what they tell me. They don't want to know about it, because if they know about it then they might be liable."

"Willful blindness," I said.

"Yes, but not for them; in your case what you're dealing with could be considered willful blindness if you're actively trying not to see what's in front of your eyes. But up at the top, or in corporate anyway, if you don't hear about it, then there's nothing you can do about it. As far as they're concerned, the stink shouldn't rise to their level under any circumstance. With so much money moving around, they know some of it's going to be fraudulent. They just manage the fraud. They pass it off, is all. They pay the fine instead of taking an audit.

"They don't want to know anything about specific fraudulent cases," he continued. "That's why what you have here on Malhotra is so interesting. It's been a while since I've found a VP who could demonstrably be proven to have had direct contact with fraudulent accounts. So even if he didn't know—"

"Of course he knew."

"Even if he didn't know, he bears liability."

I thought for a second and then asked him, "What have you been doing with all the accounts and files I've been giving to Janson?"

"Who's Janson?"

"You must know Mitch."

"I don't know him." Esperanza sat back in his chair at that point. "I don't know a Mitch Janson; that name hasn't come across my desk."

"He hasn't been giving you the files I was passing along to him?"

He just shook his head at me. I could tell where I stood with Esperanza. He was a man doing his job under the conditions as they were given to him. He didn't create the fraudulent loans, but his job wasn't as an auditor, nor was he the police. He was internally hired by the company to protect the company. No more, no less. I believed then and I believe now that as a man, he was not corrupt, but how uncorrupt can you be in a system that's begun asking you to accept fraud and to hide that fraud. If he was only allowed to hand over 10 percent of the fraudulent cases to the higher-ups who would decide what actions to take, then really his job was to mitigate the damage and try to minimize the amount of real fraud there was.

I wasn't happy about this. We sat silent for a moment. He was thumbing through the files and shaking his head. Some of the things in those files he knew about; others he had never seen.

I was thinking, "I am not supposed to see or talk about any of this fraud to anyone. Bank policy states that I have to hand my findings to the appropriate people within the company. Esperanza is only 'allowed' to report 10 percent of what fraud he finds. A known perpetrator and employee is allowed to quit without prosecution. Clients with fraudulent accounts are kept on the books. Jansen claims to know nothing. Malhotra and Jacobs assure me everything is fine. Now, I wonder, who is behind all of this and how much money are they making? How much inside the bank and how much outside? Where is the money going? If a big investigation came along right now, who would be the first one thrown in jail—that would be me—then Steve because he only reported the tip of the iceberg. But I am not going to jail; I have a tape recorder."

I broke the silence: "So she just gets to ride off into the sunset and decorate homes."

"Who's that?"

"Anjali!"

"Oh, I wouldn't put it that way." And he stopped and looked at me for a while.

"What way would you put it? We got the e-mail that she resigned to decorate houses— follow her passion."

"She quit. We brought her in to question her about some of these loans and accounts you've brought into me now. I started asking her questions, and she stood up and said, 'I don't like your fucking tone.' She got up and walked into Sanja's office. He came out after that and told us that she had to quit and was packing her things to leave. We were told not to take it any further. But it's interesting because I've gotten reports since she left that she meets with Sanja at his house on a weekly basis."

"How do you know that?"

"We have eyes. Anyway, whatever they're doing, they're certainly very close to one another."

"She's still dealing with clients. That's how she's do-ing it."

"Oh, I couldn't speculate that far, but it's possible."

I knew they were covering up. They were just trying to make this whole thing go away. He leaned into me now. His voice was self-assured. He looked at me and said, "This Sanja guy runs a crooked ship. It was never

188

like this when Morabito was here. Ever since he took over, the fraudulent activities keep piling up. But if I were you, I'd be very careful about who I let in on this stuff. I've got no idea who he's working with. And we're talking a lot of money moving through this bank, and those kind of numbers don't just come from nowhere. They don't come from selling furniture or whatever else those companies say they sell."

We stood up together. The meeting was over. But as he left he repeated himself: "We hardly ever saw any of this shit before Sanja; when Joseph was in charge it wasn't like this, but now it is."

Then he opened the door. "I'll be in touch, Mr. Cruz. You've got my card if you need to contact me."

Chapter 26

A few days later, Janson left a message that he needed to see me. He sounded friendly, which was abnormal for him because he usually sounded so stiff and robotic. He really did sound like the perfect company man. He even talked like a company memo or e-mail: "Mr. Cruz we would like to see you perform better, I believe in you and in your talent." You only have to supply the droning voice to get the picture. So when I heard him talking as if we were on friendly terms and he was just asking to go out and get a beer, I knew I was in real trouble.

It was the later part of July. I had been saving my e-mails. I was also tape recording every conversation and keeping every document that pertained to me. These bankers at HSBC had ceased to be my coworkers—and this was the hardest part to take and why the ensuing months were so difficult. It's one thing when you go to work and hate your job; it's another thing when your job hates you. In situations like these, you

191

not only have to watch your step as is normal; you also have to watch out for management taking you out of the game.

I walked into Janson's office in Melville fully expecting to be reprimanded or suspended, or God knows what. He closed the door behind me and didn't say hello or good morning.

"What the fuck did you go to security for without my permission? I didn't tell you that you could."

"You were out on vacation."

His face was turning red. I could have understood his anger if I thought he had been involved in the fraud. But there was no link to him at all in any of the paperwork. And since I knew when he was hired and where he had been hired from, I didn't believe there was any way on the planet that he was involved at all. It's possible, but less than likely. His anger then was just about control and punishment. I've noticed in my years in business that with some people contracts and leadership have nothing to do with fulfillment and profit and success. They see the world through the lens of the inquisitor, and they believe their function, as part of their motivational technique, is to punish people; to twist them and shame them and make them otherwise squirm. If you breach protocol in some minor way, then their job is to punish you. They want to crack the whip. I think it boils down to the fact that their idea of a team is more like a team of horses that need whipping to drive them on than a team of humans who need incorporation.

But another aspect of this personality type is they usually back off when you push back. They accept the whipping as they think you should. But he wasn't letting go, and he wasn't backing down.

"How dare you try to go around me, Cruz!"

"You weren't here."

"Then you go to Sanja or Dan Alton; nowhere does the HSBC handbook say that you go outside of management on your own to get to security. You know that. Use the fucking pipeline."

He was steaming mad. I felt a smirk come across my face, but I quickly erased it. I didn't want to tempt him even more, but I knew something he didn't.

"I didn't go outside the pipeline."

"Like hell you didn't."

"I went to Duggan."

"Duggan is not your fucking manager anymore. Do you get that?"

"But I didn't. You, Sanja, and a few of the others took overlapping vacations, and on one of the days, that put Duggan in charge. I had found more fraud over at Northport and some more out in Commack."

"You and this fraud."

"Well, I didn't make it up."

"I know you didn't, but…"

"But what?" I asked him. He sighed at this point. It's like he knew everything about the fraud that I did, but he wanted me to pretend I didn't see it. Judging from what Esperanza at security told me, if he was told to suppress about 90 percent of the cases, then maybe we were all supposed to do the same thing, from managers to SBRMs and on. But it was a memo I never got and hadn't signed on for. And I was fairly certain it wasn't in my job description to enable money launder-ing by covering up as much of it as I could.

Though Janson didn't say any of this, he wanted to. He acknowledged the fraud, but he didn't want me to acknowledge it. He certainly didn't want me going around him to report what he was supposed to have been reporting. But the rules didn't matter if we all ig-nored them, and that was the point. By going around him, I put the fraud on record without his consent. Not only that, he might become liable for what he had kept quiet about before. Now we were in a blame game. Just like Lou said, "Cover your ass."

But then Janson became livid. He flipped out, "How dare you go behind my back! I've had it up to here with you, Cruz."

"I did my job, and I did it exactly like the handbook says I'm supposed to. I had already informed you that there was fraud.

"You didn't inform me."

"I told you there was fraud."

"You told me nothing."

"I've been telling you since I got to that branch there was fraud. Why don't you just pull me out of there?"

"That's what this is, huh, Cruz? A game so you get sent back to your old ground."

"I can't continue to do my job to the levels required of me if one-third of the accounts are fraudulent."

"You better keep up your numbers; that's all I have to say John."

"HSBC policy is to remove the people who find the fraud from the branches where they found it."

"I don't want to hear about it anymore. Just get out. And no more excuses." Then he stopped. I looked him and he said: "But there's another thing before you go."

He spoke in a different tone now. He was calm; he seemed to smile from his office chair. "There's some talk of a sexual harassment charge against you from about two months ago, John. That's actually why I called you in here, but then I caught wind of you going to security."

"What do you mean, some talk?"

"I'm not allowed to give you the details."

"You can't give me the details to a sexual harassment charge against me? Where was it?"

He just shook his head: "Is there anything you want to tell me about it?"

"Is there anything I want to tell you about what? I don't even know when or where this was supposed to have happened."

"Is there anything you want to tell me about these charges, John? This is serious." But he was almost mocking me.

"*No.* I have to know where and what they are in order to give an opinion about them."

"Well, Maria Duran over in HR is handling the charge."

"Can I talk with her?" I asked. "It seems important that I be able to have some input."

"This is an ongoing investigation, John. Ms. Duran will be in touch with you soon."

I closed his door gently as I left, in spite of the rage I felt boiling up in me. I wanted to slam the door so hard it came off its hinges and pinned Mitch to the wall. I made it out of his office, out of his hallway, out of the lobby, and crossed the parking lot. I continued on beyond the security camera and past the purple cone-flowers and orange tiger lilies.

A few blocks away, I pulled into a McDonalds. Taking the left hand turn into the lot the car behind me got so close it almost hit me. It was a blue Cadillac. I shook it off and ordered breakfast; an Egg McMuffin, hash browns, and a coffee, black. I usually didn't eat this much. I stayed away from fast food all together. But I had gained nearly ten pounds since taking on this new position.

In the parking lot I tried to calm down. I was angry. I ate the egg and sausage sandwich. Now there was this charge of sexual harassment to deal with. What a bunch of nonsense. And they thought they were not required to tell me what was alleged or where it hap-pened or when? There was no sexual harassment, no where, no how; not by me. Janson just threw the accu-sation out there to let it fester in my mind. That was all. The accusation itself was enough to sicken me.

Now it was percolating. It didn't matter what I did. I was out. Everyone had a vested interest in covering up because they could retain their jobs. In that way everyone shared the blame. In that way a major bank engaged in fraud and money laundering, and no one did anything about it. And if they did, the bank merely paid a fine and continued about its business.

Chapter 27

By August I just wanted to keep a low profile. I knew I had done nothing wrong, and quitting would only help build their case against me. So I resolved that while I wouldn't turn a blind eye, I would keep a low profile. But it was too late: I was already fodder for the rumor mill. Early in the month, I had the opportunity to chat with the SBRM from Valley Stream. I didn't know him well, as he had only become an SBRM within the past few months. I had seen him at meetings and in passing at the Melville office. Summer was dragging along, and a lot of our team was on vacation. Melville was somewhat peaceful then, conducive for a little bonding time. This SBRM was a big guy with dirty blond hair that he kept a little longer than most men in banking. We seemed to hit it off pretty well. I decided to tell him a bit of what I had found. I thought he might be someone I could commiserate with.

"Yeah, that sounds about right," he said. "But I wouldn't worry about it."

I felt my heart sink when he said that, but I brought up the fact of how much fraud there actually was in some of the branches in my territories.

"Yeah, they were a little out of control out in Commack and East Northport for a while. Everyone knew that. They originated a lot of bad loans. Usually the customers who began their accounts out that way and wound up doing business in other branches were all wet. I've seen it for a while now. But I usually don't say anything about it. And if I do, I just put it in an e-mail and move on. Man, what you're doing's not really the way to go about it."

He was making me uneasy. I could feel my forehead get clammy. I had thought he was someone to confide in. But now it turned out that he knew and didn't care.

"But you weren't the SBRM at the branch where all this stuff was uncovered," I said. "What would you have done then?" He didn't have an answer to this question right away. His attitude worked fine if you just found a few fraudulent accounts here and there and they were originating out of branches that weren't your responsibility, but when they were your accounts it was a different story. And then he said: "Honestly, I'd probably find another job."

I was thinking about finding a new job, too. I had begun preliminary talks with a lawyer right after my verbal warning. The attorney's advice, without having looked too much into the case, was that I stay put. "Don't quit," he said. "Don't quit no matter what happens, and do whatever they tell you to do. If you keep finding fraud, keep shuffling it through the channels, get it in an e-mail. But make sure you get it noted. You might also think about talking with the Suffolk County DA. If there really is such a volume of money coming through as you say there is, then these are big players you're talking about."

I didn't like this idea right off the bat. "I'm less concerned about who's initiating the accounts from the outside than with who's working the fraud from the inside and making the bank corrupt."

"But that's no way to look at it," he said. "You had better be concerned about who owns these accounts, because if you keep making noise like you are, they're going to be very interested in you." He was right. I had already been threatened by one customer, although that wasn't over exposing fraud but rather at my refusal to give him a loan he didn't qualify for.

In truth, I had ceased to be sure of anything. Just two months ago, or less, I had a career. I had both a strong history and a bright future. Now I didn't see how I would make it through the week. With every account I turned in that was fraudulent, my balances were dragged downward and I was held accountable. I had already removed 40 to 50 percent from East Northport's balances. In Commack I had done the same.

I had been getting phone calls to my house in the middle of the night for at least two weeks now. These phone calls were from unlisted numbers. Summertime at my house is family time: beach, cookouts, bike rides, and movies on those sweltering nights. My house was not so much fun anymore. I was tired and nervous. I was worried for my safety. As if it wasn't hard enough to get a good night's sleep, someone was calling my house at all hours. I was sure it was one of my friends at the bank. I reported it to the annoyance call bureau at the phone company. I was supposed to answer the phone, and then when I got hung up on I was to hit #58 and they would trace the call. But after a week, they were unable to get a "good number." I unplugged the landline at night after that. Cells were off or on vibrate.

It was no better at work either. Branch managers like Mack Johnson wanted me out, or worse. Management wanted nothing to do with me. My day-to-day life was oppressive. In a situation like this, in a company this large, the rumor mill is gigantic. Coworkers begin treating you differently so that you don't know if it's because they think you are the latest fool or a hero they're afraid to be near. Either way it's lonely.

Chapter 28

It was just a few days later that I saw Angela Martin again in East Northport. She wanted to talk to me about the fraud she had found, and about how her notary stamp had been duplicated and her signature forged. First I was headed down to the basement of the branch looking up the paperwork on some corporation out of Montauk, New York. There was a large storage area used for files for copies of documents on loans we originated and also closed deposit accounts. It was sterile and clean for a storage area in an old basement. Everything was permeated by the dead off-white and hum of fluorescents. When I got to the bottom of the stairs, I was surprised to see two men standing in and among the files cabinets talking. They were HSBC's internal auditors. One of them looked up when he saw me.

"How are you?" he said.

"I'm fine." I had met them once before. "Steve and Mark, right?"

"We are," the one with the dark hair said. "Steve."

Mark looked up over his bifocals and nodded to me. Then he went back to work.

"I'm John Cruz. I think we've met before over in Melville."

"Nice to meet you again, John. Do you need something from me?"

"Well, in fact, yes. I've been finding what I believe is fraud and money laundering out of this branch and a few others. And if I'm seeing it, I know you are. What happens to it?"

"Well you have to be more specific," Steve said; the other one didn't bother to lift his head.

"I mean, when a company has no tax returns or incomplete information, what do you do with it?"

"Well it depends really, but if what you're asking is why we don't report it, the reason is simple. We try and keep fraud down internally, but at the least we want to know about it. We don't open our books to anyone, ever, if it can be avoided; we just pay the fines if it comes to that. It's simple enough that way. The company itself has a huge account set aside to just pay fines and judgments rather than open up."

Mark perked up at that moment to say: "We simply report internally if we find it."

"But do you look at the numbers?" I persisted. "I mean, if someone is getting a loan based on earnings they can't justify with tax returns, or companies with bogus tax ID numbers getting loans that are charged off in six months' time."

"We don't usually dig that deep unless we're asked to. We basically just make sure the paperwork is all there. If not, then we flag it. As to the charge-offs, we only pay attention to that when the number the branch has committed rises to a certain level, or we have a specific reason."

Then I asked him, "You must be seeing all the stuff I'm seeing, all these accounts out of here are bogus. The information is fake. The only real number is the amount of money coming in through PayPal, wire transfers, etc. There's millions a day coming just through a few branches, I've seen it. That's big numbers for just a few branches. Stuff like this can bring a bank down."

"I wouldn't worry about that; we don't. Those numbers are there; where they come from doesn't really matter. In the end, we can afford to pay the fines. The bank has some two billion set aside to defend itself with. Justice never goes to trial; besides, they want the money. As long as we can pay, we can play."

I took the file I needed, and they went back about their work, which I guess was to find errors not to report. They worked simply as another layer of bank protection. Whereas branch managers and relationship managers could only expose so much fraud, and security was expected to sit on 90 percent of what they did bring up, these guys went through the paperwork just to see if it was all there. They put a rubber stamp on most of what the BMs put out except for the most flagrant examples; even then they didn't seem to do much. They just alerted people if they thought they could get hurt.

When I went back upstairs, I ran right into Angela Martin. This time she didn't run away from me. She signaled to me in a strange and, I thought, overly clandestine way. She was like a school kid with a secret.

I met her over by the coffee machine in the customer waiting area. She asked if we could talk over lunch outside of work. Of course I agreed. But she wouldn't tell me anything until later on. She picked an Irish pub to meet at over in Port Jefferson. It was a little out of the way from Northport, but she wanted to be private.

The first thing she asked me was, "Did anyone know you were coming here?"

"No."

"Did someone follow you?"

"No," I said, but then I thought that I'd recognized the same blue Cadillac from the McDonalds in Melville. But I didn't tell Angela that. Nor did I allow myself to believe I was being followed. It wasn't a possibility I wanted to admit.

We sat down at the table. I ordered an onion soup and a cheeseburger. She had a salad. I didn't usually eat so much in the afternoons; for years I had made it a point to eat light and control my weight, but I found I was eating more now. My stress was high, and eating was comforting. And it was a different type of stress than I had ever experienced before. It wasn't the adrenaline-rush kind of stress you feel when you're startled. It wasn't the give-it-your-all kind of feeling when you're cramming for a test or finishing a report within a deadline. It wasn't even the overwhelmed-because-I-have-too-much-on-my-plate kind of stress. It was stress born of hopelessness, misery, failure, and being nearly 100 percent certain that there was not going to be a happy ending. It was waiting for the end and not being sure when or how it would come. It was stress heaped on me that I openly took on because I thought I could fix something that was beyond repair. It was stress that permeated my life, my sleep…there was no relief.

We talked over our food. I didn't want to just begin questioning her, but she came out and said her piece.

"How did you find it?" she said.

I didn't bother playing dumb. I knew what *it* was. "The first thing I found was businesses that moved more money through their accounts in a week than they were supposed to gross in a year. When I looked up their addresses, they turned out to be fake. Then I noticed your name on some of the loans. There were loans too large for a BBS's portfolio. Also, there were loans in your portfolio that I didn't believe a credit officer would ever approve." I didn't tell her that Janice had tipped me off to her.

"I've only submitted loans for up to twenty thousand dollars since I've been working here," she said.

"Well, I found well over a million in loans at least in your name. Over and over again."

"It was Anjali. She had my signature duplicated."

"I heard she does that."

"She was originating loans using my name as the requesting officer, like she was me, and she was using my stamp to notarize documents on other loans I had nothing to do with."

Those were the loans I had incomplete tax information for. Some of them began with Anjali; then went to the underwriter, who declined them; then over to the senior vice president, who underwrote them; and then Angela's notary stamp was used to finalize that all the signatures were valid. It either worked that way, or the loan was originated by Angela Martin; went to the underwriter, who declined; and was signed by Sanja and notarized by Mack out in Commack. I had a clear picture of how it worked, but I just wondered why no one was doing anything about it. This group of people had turned southern New York's branches of HSBC into a money-laundering/cash machine that loaned money to dummy companies while other companies funneled millions through them. Then the corporate structure itself protected the perpetrators. It was likely that corruption went up beyond Sanja Malhotra senior VP, and since Art Jacobs, who was above Malhotra on the regional level, had pretended like there wasn't anything to be worried about, it was a fair assumption to make. But I had no proof, at least not yet.

Angela wasn't finished saying her piece. She had remained quiet long enough and seemed to be happy to have some one to commiserate with. "She never said anything to me. But I happened to come across something in the computer one day that said how much I had loaned out. I showed Janice, and she had me to go outside of Anjali. I wound up at security, and they told me to just be quiet about it and that they would handle it. After that, I moved around a little bit, but then it was back to the branches."

"Who, Esperanza?"

"Yeah. It's just a big open joke. That whole branch is fraudulent. All the numbers come off crooked accounts. I know just enough to know the difference. I'm telling you because you're pressing the issue, but I don't know what you can do. I don't know how far you can get this way."

I didn't know how far I would get going this way either, but I was left with few options. "What else should I do?" I asked her. "Every account they give me's bullshit. I've actually got to deal with clients who don't exist or who have five thousand accounts and forty credit cards under different business names. Or I find my name on loans linked to accounts attached to businesses that actually are out of business. Every type of fraud there is and that I've ever seen is being run out of this branch."

She seemed to smile at me now. "Everyone knows it. It's no secret. But if you want to keep working, you just keep quiet and show up to work. The paychecks come like they're supposed to."

"Yeah, but you don't have to eat this stuff. It all has to go through me. And Janson wants to hold me to it. There's no better way to see your performance go down then to report fraud here. That's one of the ways it's been going on so long. Since I spoke up, I've had verbal reprimands about my performance, and now I know another written one is coming after this. Nobody wants to take a hit to their bottom line," I said.

"I know, if I had to deal with it like you do, I'd probably quit, but it's easy enough for me."

"Except they had to charge off over a million dollars in your loans. That's still there; it didn't go away."

"I know. I'm glad you found it; now at least some-body knows. But what was I supposed to do? I didn't know the bank was crooked like this. I figured maybe in a local bank you'd have people getting away with this stuff, but multinational corporations are supposed to be watching their people like hawks, you know. I just wanted a job. I just signed on for a paycheck and to work my way up the ladder; I can't go and hurt my own career. When I saw the fraud, I reported it to the guy who was there before Janson; he sent me to security. They tell me, 'Thank you, we'll handle it, that's that. If my manager was signing loans in my name, then it's on the record that I reported it, so when it all comes down they can see that I was not involved. Other than that, I don't care what they do. It's their money. That's the one thing I've learned. It's their money because they make it up, and they can do whatever they want with it."

"You might even get a promotion," I said.

"I just might, and you know what, I deserve it. I de-serve a promotion for having to put up with this."

"Why not go to the police?"

"Did it work for you with your notary stamp? Do you really think I would have any better luck with this? All I would do is lose my job, and for what?" She was right, and we both knew it. She was the lowly bank-ing specialist whom Anjali was taking advantage of, but she was smart, and she knew enough to protect herself and keep her head down. I envied her in that moment. She was safe, and she could stay safe.

"But I'll tell you…if you're really going to keep pushing this…"

"I don't have a choice."

"Then you should look into Daryl Rupka. He was working with Anjali, and she thinks I'm too stupid to know what happened, but he told me. He hates her, and he hates Sanja for what they wanted from him. His business is selling gift cards for small businesses. He was my client. And when Anjali got a hold of him, he left the bank. He told me that he wouldn't work with her, and that I should watch myself; that was it. I know what they wanted him to do, but you'd better hear it from him."

Chapter 29

She had given me a number and a name. I called the number and spoke with Daryl Rupka. I told him who I was. He almost hung up.

"No, I don't want any," he said.

But I kept him on the phone: "I'm the new VP and senior business relationship manager with HSBC bank. Anjali's no longer with the bank, and I wanted to reach out to former clients to offer my assistance."

"Have fun."

"I'd like the opportunity to talk…to understand what happened."

He told me that I could meet with him in New Jersey at his office. I wanted nothing to do with going to Jersey. It could take forever and a day to get there from out on the Island. But, miserable drive or not, I agreed.

We met at a small unit he kept in an office park. As Angela had described, he ran a business that sold gift cards to small businesses. He facilitated the small businesses in the establishment of credit lines through which the cards operated. He would set these relation-ships up with the major credit card companies: Visa, Amex, Master, Discover. I could see why Anjali would want to use him.

He led me inside to a room that looked out over the highway. He didn't offer me a seat. Instead he walked close, then closer. He was in my face. My stomach rolled over. "You wearing a fuckin' wire?"

I shrugged.

"Where's your fucking recorder?" he said, and start-ed rummaging through my pockets. He found it in no time in my jacket pocket. He pulled it out and turned it off. Then he tossed it on the table, causing the battery door to open. The battery danced across the table onto the floor.

"Is that the only one?"

"Yeah."

"All you fucking bank people wear wires? Do you people fuck up so much and tell so many lies that you can't remember your own shit? Or is your game to im-plicate then intimidate your so-called clients?" I didn't respond. After all, what was there to say?

"I'll tell you what I know, but you're not going to record one word. This shit isn't coming back to me." He sat down and began his story. "We're talking ma-jor fucking money here, and people kill for that kind of money." He watched me for a few seconds to see how I'd respond. Then he started talking: "Angela told you about me?"

"Yeah."

"Why?"

"When I took over a few months ago…" I couldn't believe it had really been such a short time. It felt like ten years, and it felt like one long never ending miserable day. And it wasn't over yet. "I came to the branch and started to find irregularities. Anjali wouldn't cooperate with me; she wouldn't give me access to her clients. My job is to deepen the relationships those clients already have with HSBC. When she eventually and reluctantly takes me to a meet a client it's to prove that his tax returns are real. Only, he's got two sets. Then he tells me to 'do what the fuck she tells me to do.'"

At that point Daryl started laughing. He laughed not so much at me but with me. It was a heartier laugh than you would expect from such a slight man. I felt some of my tension easing and noticed the intelligent confidence in his eyes. He laughed out loud for a bit longer. Then he chuckled. "Nothing would surprise me with her. Let me ask you, did you report the things you found to anyone at the job?"

"Of course."

"And what'd you get for it?"

"I think I'll be fired by the end of the summer." Actually I was wrong about the timing; they continued to toy with me like a cat with a mouse for a few months longer than that. My guess is that HR wanted to use this time to create numerous and documented causes.

He must have enjoyed hearing that I was sure I'd be fired. It started him into a new fit of laughter. Then he started to reveal his experience, "I deal with banks, credit card companies, all the time, and these people you work for are as corrupt as they come. From what Anjali divulged when she was pitching her proposition to me, they're compartmentalized in such a way that corruption is relative. Their enforcement depends on how much money is at stake. I mean, a bank like that didn't thrive in Hong Kong for no reason, right? They know how to hide things. I mean, they were in fact founded to help finance trade in the late eighteen hundreds. That was trade between Hong Kong and Shanghai. What were they trading? Opium. Then it was legal. They act now as if it's still legal. They legitimize themselves by paying fines, which to them are just a part of the cost of doing business. They're not here to play by any rules they don't have to play by."

"What did she want from you?"

"You see what I do here? I set up lines of credit for gift cards. We do a lot of small business, but sometimes we get the larger local chains, hotels, sporting goods, malls, that sort of thing. Anjali knows what I do."

"How did you come to bank with an HSBC branch out in Northport if you work all the way out here?"

"Easy, I do a lot of business out in Manhattan; some of my clients banked with her, they gave me her name, and we started doing business."

"You were looking for a soft bank?"

"I was looking to have a relationship with a major international bank. With other banks it's tough to get some transactions done quickly. You know, you're a manger, but they can't do anything. I needed someone who was flexible, but not crooked. I didn't want a cartel; I just needed a banker who could do business across borders and who was on my side; besides, other banks use HSBC to move their international currency. So why not go to the source?"

I nodded at him, and he continued talking. I was intrigued, but I could guess what he was going to say next.

"She wanted to use my accounts to launder money. She wanted me to sell her large blocks of charged gift cards, and sell hundreds of them or so to various businesses she had through the bank. The companies would buy gift cards for whatever reason with five hundred to one thousand dollars on each of them."

"Who would they go to?"

"I have no idea; we didn't get that far. I make enough money, and I have no issues with the IRS; everything here smells like roses, so I didn't need to create problems for myself where none existed. My guess would be that this is one way to move laundered drug money out of the country. It's not really a guess. The government watches us like a hawk because these cards represent such a simple way to move money. You put it in gift cards. Who's going to stop you boarding a plane with fifteen credit cards in you wallet? They don't even check your wallet at customs. Everyone's got a bunch of cards now. Holding various credit cards will not arouse any suspicion. Or, you just FedEx the fucking things to wherever. The money goes into multiple American companies or accounts from wherever the fuck it comes from in the world. It comes in through PayPal or electronic transfers straight from Indonesia or Shanghai or Manhattan or Delaware. From these

American accounts, if you want to get it out of the country, then you have to buy things or transfer, but another good option is to put sums on multiple gift cards."

"Yeah, but one company can only buy so many gift cards."

"If you're really looking at the paperwork, they don't have one company or two or twenty; they have four hundred companies with multiple accounts in twenty-five or sixty different branches. You get it. It's a shell game. Money can be divided up into little bits, separated to a thousand places, and then channeled back to some account somewhere in Colombia or Brazil or Britain. And they can't trace it across the border. You get it?"

"But you can't move a billion dollars with it."

"Maybe not with gift cards, or all at once, but it's a trickle. And if you're laundering money, then you've got to be diversified anyhow. Besides, do you think the feds can see into who's cashing AmEx gift cards in Colombia or Mexico or Brazil? They check you for carrying cash; they don't give a shit about plastic. As long as you're not carrying stacks of it, it doesn't matter what form it takes."

"But they'd catch you."

"Oh, they'd catch me, all right. Despite what Mr. fucking Malhotra promised. They'd get me. That's why I walked away. But your branch manager didn't seem to worry about being caught. And that's exactly what was going on. I've got no idea about whose account she's got or what they put through that branch, but I do know she was looking to make a deal where she transfers money into gift cards on an industrial level. She told me I would take a percent of what comes through, just like it's legitimate; only sooner or later, no matter how fragmented it is or how many accounts they divide the money into, someone will catch on."

I didn't know what to say to him.

Then he said: "That Indian you work for is evil. He's fucking evil."

"Sanja."

"Yeah, watch your back."

On the drive back from Jersey, I was thinking about Economics 1 at SCCC in Selden. We had a lecture once about the barter system and how it developed into a monetary system. "I'll fix your shoe for a chicken." Something like that. "I don't have a chicken, but I'll give you a loaf of bread." "OK, I'll fix your shoe for two loaves of bread and then trade the bread for someone else's chicken." Some genius of the time realized that this is a very inefficient way of doing business. They invented the concept of money and assigned an agreed-upon value to it. Special rocks with markings chinked into them represented the physical money.

Some guy comes along and has a bunch of fake rocks and trades them for all of the chickens and bread and goats and blankets. He has all the stuff, and the money rocks are worthless. Fraud was invented along time ago.

Chapter 30

Janson had scheduled an appointment with me to discuss my midyear performance review. He looked stern leaning against the doorjamb to his office. He had a look of great disappointed in me. I knew what was coming. I knew he was about to dump a bad midyear evaluation on me, and that our conversation was a merely a formality. It was, after all, his show, and he gave a fine performance.

"You know, John, I *really* believe in your ability to succeed; you just have to increase your pipeline and make all the calls you're supposed to make." It's funny that he was saying exactly these words to me. He had handed me the printout of my midyear review, and it used exactly the same language he was using now; it was like he was reading from a script—the script for bad managers. It felt like he was patronizing me. He knew there was fraud, and so did I, but he wasn't going to admit it. I also wondered if he knew I had a tape recorder. He might have suspected as much. If he looked in my file at all he would know that I had dealt with fraud for years and knew how to protect myself. So I was protecting myself, and he was protecting himself. And this was where we stood. If I was going to continue to see fraud, my performance was going to continue to decline both in real numbers and in the minds of the senior executives.

This whole episode was going to go away. The executives would deal with it like it was an aberration. It would be buried in the accounting category "chargeoffs of bad debt." HSBC Bank USA, has a national charter and is therefore regulated by the OCC (Office of the Comptroller of Currency.) In the case of an audit with negative findings, fines would be levied by the Department of the Treasury. But that still left me holding the bag locally. I was being instructed to turn a blind eye. I had to go on dealing with clients that were criminals. Years of bank experience and years of mandated Bank Secrecy Act training taught me that I must report when I see suspicious activity; if the person(s) to whom I make my report do not take appropriate action then I must report it to their supervisor; and so on. If I do not do this according to the BSA then I am committing "willful Blindness" and I can expect to be fined personally and be subject to prosecution. This was drilled into every banker's head and it still is.

At HSBC we all shared the knowledge of what was going on. We had to share the guilt; that's what my supervisors wanted. Maybe one or two people got in trouble, while everyone else, including the bank, went on conducting business as usual. It was a fine plan;

only I didn't want to share in the guilt. I didn't want to go along with the fraud. I certainly didn't want to share a jail cell with Mitch Janson.

And I didn't know how to play by their rules. I didn't care to turn a blind eye. I might have walked away if this Janson character hadn't been hell bent on getting his way, but his way included keeping me in these branches and having me actually boost their performance. Had he removed me from the situation once I reported it to him, and had he assured me that everything would be properly reported, and had he arranged for the fraudulent accounts to be closed, things could have continued on without my knowledge. He didn't care what I discovered. He didn't care that my performance was affected (affected! It was destroyed) by the fraud and the money laundering. He didn't care that I couldn't sleep at night, or that I felt physically ill nearly every day, or that my life had been threatened, or that it seemed that half my businesses were frauds.

He continued droning on in that awful way, reciting a canned motivational speech so that he looked supportive when I was fired. All the while, I was trying to decide who else I could report to while waiting for advice from my attorney. Then I spoke up, and he lost his cool in a nasty episode of screaming insults, which I am sure did not go in the file.

"What about the fraud?" I asked.

Before he got angry he looked at me over his glasses. He had beady little brown eyes that made him look like a bird of prey. I waited for him to respond, but after a moment he looked back down and continued his speech about my lack of performance.

I asked him again: "What about the fraud at Commack and East—"

"There is no fucking fraud. I don't want to hear about the fraud."

"It isn't there, or you don't want to hear about it?"

"I'm sick of you, John, you know that? That branch was a numbers machine before you got there, a fucking gold mine, and you're just not keeping up the trend. And if you can't do it, I'll get someone who will."

"The numbers were fraudulent. They were based on crooked accounts."

"Your performance has not been what we expected."

He wasn't going to drop the routine. I reached into my briefcase and handed him a stack of papers. They were more files I had uncovered over the last several weeks that were without a doubt fraudulent. The first sign was that all of the accounts were handled by the same accountant Ranj Sekar. As soon as I saw his name I hardly had to look any further.

He shuffled the paperwork to the side as if it were contagious. Then he handed me the midyear review. I read his comments, which basically paralleled what he had already said to me. I wasn't producing the numbers. I hadn't made enough meetings, etc., etc., etc. When I finished reading and looked up at him, he said:

"John, as usual on these reviews we allow you to have a few comments. Would you mind going to your desk and writing a few comments? And please remember these are not just seen by me."

He e-mailed the file to my account, and I went to my desk and filled in the comments:

This is to make it known that I could not disagree with the EPM's opinion of my performance more strongly. There are several major issues preventing my achievement of the level of performance required. Beginning with my time in Carle Place, there were incidences of fraud that went largely unnoticed until an employee was arrested. Her arrest had an impact on branch performance, but since being installed as SBRM in Suffolk as of March 23, 2009, I have encountered repeated incidences of fraud. Both branch managers have knowledge of the fraud, and the East Northport manager was removed without reason, but presumably, as she herself said to me, she was removed because 80 percent of her loans were in default. I have brought the evidence to the attention of the EPM repeatedly and to the head of security. I have encountered only opposition. At least 15 to 20 percent of the East Northport and Commack accounts are demonstrably fraudulent or have totally insufficient paperwork.

"You're not fucking handing that in," Janson said from his desk. I could hear over my shoulder at the computer terminal I was sitting at. I had just e-mailed it to him. I walked into his office. His face was red. "If you won't fill it out properly, then I will do it for you," and he proceeded to delete what I wrote and add his own corporate speak: "I will do better. I believe in my manager. We will work together. Thank you."

But when he e-mailed it back to me for my approval I cut out the comment he had added and pasted my original comments back into the form. I returned it to him, but he made no further comment. I knew when I hit enter that I was declaring open war. The midyear appraisal was a permanent HR record, and therefore my comments would be around the corporation for a while. Firing me directly afterward would look incredibly bad for Janson. I knew that he would have to wait, and that he would need to build a case against me. The case against them, on the other hand, was already clear, only no one would listen to me…yet.

Chapter 31

I was headed from the Commack branch where I had just had it out with Mack Johnson. He had told me that I had no right sending any of his documents up to Janson.

"You fucking asshole," he said. "Who the fuck do you think you are?" He was standing, pointing his finger into my chest.

"Back off me."

"You've got no right handing this stuff over to Janson. What the fuck does he know about what I'm doing?"

"Look, I find fraud, I move it up the chain. Otherwise it's mine."

"What do you want, Cruz?"

I didn't answer him. What I wanted was to go home to my wife and kids. I'd had another long day and didn't need to deal with this guy yelling at me because he was running a corrupt branch. The first reaction of someone caught red-handed is almost always to point the finger right back at the person who caught them, and this reaction holds true all the way back to preschool days. The stakes just increase as we get older. This was why Lou was so adamant with me to cover my ass and never be complacent. When you go onto someone else's field and catch them up to no good, you'd better be prepared for their retaliation. And there's always retaliation. The people who commit these types of crimes, in my experience, are also usually the people who go tit for tat and see everything as a threat and an affront. So when you catch them out in the open doing what they're not supposed to be doing, they don't view you like you were just doing your job; no, they look at you like a rival gang member. And you can usually tell who's on their team by the people who turn on you when you point out the fraud. These, of course, are the people who have something to lose and know it.

Johnson started screaming at me again, but I cut him off. "Listen, Mack, it's not my job to let you get away with pulling this shit. You got that right. Don't turn straw companies in, and I won't turn them over. I'm not going to handle accounts I know are fake and just turn a blind eye." He started to talk, but I cut him off again. He looked furious. He was red in the face, but I was relieved when he backed down, "Not only that, but I'm not going listen to you yell at me for doing what I'm supposed to do."

I walked out on him. I was furious, too, but I didn't want to continue with a screaming match. It was a waste of time and energy. I didn't dare say what I really felt about him or what I knew he was doing. It may sound silly in hindsight, but I didn't let him know exactly how little I thought of him, because I was protecting myself. I knew he hated me, but I didn't want to infuriate him more. It feels a little naïve now, but I think the principle is at least sound; I was trying not to make him hate me more. If I've learned anything in my life, I know that people will hate you all the more when you hurt them with words. If I were to have told him that he was a lowlife reptile who had turned his branch into a criminal enterprise, his fury world have been twice what it was now. And when people hate you, there's no telling what they'll do.

In hindsight it wouldn't have mattered what I said to him at that point anyway. Anything short of running his mother over with my car on purpose couldn't have made him loathe me more than he did. He looked at me like I was a rat. The reality was that we worked for corporate America, and that *Godfather* stuff was his own fantasy. Nevertheless, he would soon show me just how much anger and revenge he really was capable of.

I didn't miss a chance to go to the gym even on a hot and humid August afternoon. Even despite this fact, I had still gained nearly twenty ponds by this point. By the time of my termination, my weight gain would be nearly 35 pounds. But, along with fast food, working out cleared my head. And after having it out with Mack, I decided to go and let out some stress. When I finished I headed to the locker rooms. On the way, I noticed a man looking at me as if he recognized me from somewhere. The way he was looking at me made me think he was going to follow me into the locker room. It was just a feeling I had, and for a second I laughed at myself, but the feeling was strong enough that I didn't bother to shower or change; I just took the bag of clean clothes from my locker and left the building as quickly as I could. The guy looked menacing. It might have been nothing. But that's what fear can do to you. Suddenly your nice life is full of anxiety and shadows. In the car ride on the way home my phone rang. I picked it up.

"Where are you? I'm with the Suffolk County police department, and I've got some questions I'd like to ask you, Mr. Cruz. Where are you? I want to come see you. I want to see you now."

"Who is this?"

"Where the fuck are you, John?"

"What's your name?"

"Don't be a fuckin' asshole all your life."

"Excuse me?"

"Keep fucking around and you're gonna be hurt. You understand that, John? You're gonna be coming out of a locker room or coming out of the McDonald's and someone's gonna break your fuckin' legs. Get the message?"

"What's your phone number? Let me call you back, officer."

He hung up. Their attempt at intimidation was stupid, almost laughable. It hadn't gone off like in the movies at all. I wasn't even afraid. But it did frighten me on another level, which I thought about as I drove home. I wondered who the bigger players were in the laundering scheme and how far they were really will-ing to go to protect their profits.

I decided to call a childhood friend of mine who was on the Suffolk County police force and get some advice. When I filled him in and got to the name of Mack Johnson in Commack, he stopped me.

"Mack Johnson?" he asked.

"He works at the bank out in Commack. He's the branch manger there."

"Well," he said, "if it's the same Johnson family I'm thinking of, then they got family on the job up and down the Suffolk and Nassau County police depart-ments. I wouldn't be surprised if it really was one of them. Of course, they're not gonna leave their names. I mean, maybe it is and maybe it isn't. But this guy you're talking about comes from a whole family of cops."

"It would have to be that way, wouldn't it?" I said.

"What do you mean?"

"I mean that of course the guy I find involved in massive bank fraud and money laundering isn't just on his own; his whole family's on the police force."

"Watch out, John. It's not pretty out there. Trust me on that."

Chapter 32

After being threatened by a "Suffolk County police officer," or somebody impersonating one, I decided it was
time to take the advice of my attorney and file a report
with the DA. Part of me was afraid to go to the police
because I was afraid of how explosive this might become. Even if I could succeed in getting through the
"blue wall," I would be concerned about some retaliation later down the road. And if I blew the lid off it and
law enforcement got involved, then people were going to jail. It was just as simple as that.

For so long I had clung to the idea that the company would take care of it. Instead, they decided they
would take care of the problem by taking care of the
person who had discovered it.

So I went to the DA's Office in Hauppauge, New
York, according to my attorney's advice. I had a discussion with a woman behind the reception counter. She
asked me to wait. I felt nervous, sickly, anxious. A young
man came out. I didn't get his name. He escorted me

behind the reception area. Shortly after ...on began, I produced for him some copies of my documentation for his review. He asked questions, and as my story began to unfold, he stopped me.

"Wait a minute," he said. "This is out of my league. I thought this was going to be something minor. Let me get my boss."

He stood up and left. A few minutes later, an older man came in. He held his hand out to introduce himself. "Hi, I'm Evan Murphy."

"John Cruz."

I began explaining again what I knew from the bottom up, and showed him the documents to back it up. Most of these documents were simply copies of another file that I kept hidden along with the tape recordings I had made.

"You've got to be fucking kidding me," Evan said. Then he took a deep breath. "Let me get my partner in on this." He called in another guy. His name was Tim. He was a little bit younger. He smiled at me awkwardly as he came in. Then they started going through the files together.

"I know him," Evan said. Then they went back to looking it over. "We need more time with these; this is something we can't just look over quickly and get the whole picture. I mean, you've got page after page here. It's going to take some time to get it all sorted out."

"I know."

"I can't believe you saved all this stuff."

"Well first, it's exactly what you're supposed to do in this position, and second, they put me there and just expected me to take a loss on all of these accounts. Maybe one or two, but not this. I'm not part of it, and I don't want to be."

Then Evan said, "Well, Mr. Cruz, I am familiar with some of the names in those files you have. You've got drug and terrorist money laundering here, and I don't know what else. This is just a piece of it, but still a big piece. You've got to be careful. Does the bank know you're here?"

"No."

"Good. Keep it that way. And don't let anyone else know you were here. You've got a lawyer, right?"

"Of course."

"Good. Just be as quiet as you can for a while, and I'll get back to you in probably a few weeks. You can call me if you want, but things like this move slow."

"What am I supposed to do now?"

"Stay there. I mean, you don't want to quit. I mean, as much as you might want to quit, it'll look bad."

Tim now spoke up: "I think it hurts your chances in the case of a lawsuit."

Evan looked at Tim, and he was quiet. "Like I was saying," Evan went on, "just keep punching the clock. Whatever they tell you to do, as long as it's not against the law, do it. When you find fraud, document it. That's really all you can do right now."

I left our meeting that day feeling as though someone had finally heard me. I felt that no matter what happened now, my case was in the right hands. I could endure no matter how they wanted to treat me.

Chapter 33

It was about a month later in the early autumn, and I was still waiting to hear back from the Suffolk County DA, Evan Murphy. I had made several calls to his office, but so far he hadn't been able to move the case forward. He told me that he had a few interesting leads, and the names of clients to talk to. He ended every conversation by telling me that he would get back to me, but that in the meantime I should feel free to contact him to see how his case was progressing.

"I think I can help you, but you've got to give me time," he said to me. "I know the position you're in; trust me, I do. It's not easy to stand up against shit like this, and I know you just didn't know what else to do. But just hang tight. What's it like there now?"

"It's not fun. I don't know why they haven't just fired me. I know my segment leader can't wait to get rid of me."

"Honestly, John," he said, "they don't want it to look like they got rid of you because you pointed out fraud.

They need a paper trail that shows they fired you for performance reasons."

"What's that leave me to do?"

"Just hang on, I'll see what traction I can get."

And so I hung on. Every time I had to talk to management, I assumed they were going to fire me. But they didn't. It's hard to live when you know the executioner is standing over you. I wanted them to just hurry up and get it over with. The anticipation was much worse than any other aspect. I lived with the feeling of impending doom. All I could do was wait and carry on living life as close to normal as I could make it. The more time they kept me hanging, the more they increased my exposure and could build a negative case against me. I hated the game. And I hated that my job had suddenly become one. I was playing Russian roulette with my reputation and career. Click and you're safe; bang and you're dead, but every new day was a new round where they got to spin the cylinder and pull the trigger on me.

In my lowest moments, I would just remember how far I had come. I would remember my mother on her deathbed, and the scrapyard, and the trailer that I fled in the dead of night. I was in that same kind of position now. And even before Ivan took me in, I always had this basic underlying insight that I was going to make life better. I didn't know how or when, but I knew I would. I had that same belief now. I believed there was light at the end of the tunnel. I believed I was going through all this for a reason. I learned the power of the corporation over the worker, and I learned firsthand the corruption behind an international bank and its subtle contribution to worldwide money laundering. But I knew I would make it out the other side because I was prepared to go all the way, and I had the paperwork to back it up.

I believed that, just as we had left Moriches and never come back, and just as I had fallen into Ivan's hands, forever changing my life, I would leave this place behind as quickly and as permanently. It would change in the blink of an eye. I just had to hang on. It would get better. But I also knew that life could change for the worse, and while I thought I was moving in the right direction, this might be the end. So the moment I was waiting for could either make or break me. I also knew that I had a stack of evidence against the bank that was indisputable. This evidence would redeem me, no matter what the bank chose to do. And if the bank wasn't going to listen to me, then I would find someone who would, no matter if I had to shout it from the mountaintops. This would define me.

So it was in this mind frame that I made it through the end of summer and through September into October. And it was about October that DA Murphy called me to say that the case had been given over to the DA in Queens for an ongoing investigation there. And that it was no longer under his command.

"What are they doing with it?"

"I couldn't tell you. But from my end it's all over. As far as I can tell, the city is in ongoing talks with HSBC about some of its dealings in the state of New York and for its US business. From what I hear, they're close to a deal."

"A deal?" But I knew what he meant. The auditors I'd met in the basement of the branch had already explained this angle of HSBC's business. They avoided any real investigation by just paying whatever fine was leveled against them. And if I had found laundering at this level coming through over the course of a few months, and I didn't even have carte blanche, then I could only imagine how widespread the corruption actually must have been. The fine would be little more than the cost of doing business for HSBC. No one was going to go to jail. No one would face prosecution.

Wachovia was charged with "serious and systemic" violations of the US's banking regulations. They paid about $160 million in fines and forfeitures while it was proven that they had funneled money for the Sinaloa Cartel. But the key feature of the judgment was the term "systemic." This wasn't a one-time thing, or the behavior of a few bad apples within the organization; they had a system designed to handle this kind of money. In actuality they had a system designed to handle this kind of risk, and now as of spring 2011, HSBC is still in talks with the Justice Department to pay a one-billion-dollar fine. So if at $160 million your crime is systemic, what is it at a billion?

Drug dealers are people, too. Their money is just as real and needs a place to go just like everyone else's. The war down in Mexico isn't financed using gold doubloons, after all. They're just not supposed to be able to do the illegal trading through the banking system. That's exactly how they're supposed to get caught and stopped. But with all that money on the line, it's hard for banks, especially in times of recession, to turn away from the possible profit. This is true above all when the profit exceeds the fine.

This was how the game worked. I hadn't had this global insight before. It had never been so up close and personal. But as I put the phone down, I understood just why I was being treated the way I was. I was up against systemic behavior, and that system went beyond the bank into the criminal justice system, which exchanged silence for money. In other words, they don't try a case if the bank can pay the fine. You are in real trouble if the fine will put you into bankruptcy or you can't pay up; in that case you are fair game. Little banks go out of business all the time under this kind of pressure because they don't have the cash on hand to pay up. They also exercise better controls to save themselves. But when a big bank like HSBC finally makes a deal, there can't be any errant Suffolk County cases pending, or no deal.

At this point, the end of 2009, there was no deal for HSBC, but it was coming. Yet it wouldn't help me. Where was I in the deal? They were going to clip my career and not even acknowledge that I had seen what I saw. They wouldn't acknowledge that I actively worked to stop their crimes. That's what a billion dollars will get you: silence.

Happy New Year!

Chapter 34

I was working at my desk back in Melville contemplating how I had accomplished nothing but making enemies when Janson called me into talk about the issues I had been having. He began with the same old pep talk I had gotten used to hearing by now, but rather than perk me up, it only depressed me. He rambled on about how I had the capabilities to achieve and perform well above my peers in this competitive market. And while I had not consistently delivered expected results, I would be able to do so with proper execution; so on and so forth. His was the ludicrous optimism of a maniacal camp counselor who wants you to fail and buries you with encouragement. All words from the manual without any real support or advocacy for me, and exactly the opposite sentiment.

"And as for the sexual harassment claim against you…"

I perked up at this. "Can you give me any information about it?" I said.

241

"I still can't say other than that it was a female teller from East Northport who is no longer employed with the bank."

As soon as he said that, I knew exactly who he was talking about. "Amala," I said.

"I'm not at liberty to answer you. I might have already said more than I should have."

"You know that's Anjali's cousin, right?" I had a sudden memory of having been introduced to Amala. I remembered clearly because afterwards Anjali told me that her cousin's name meant "purity."

"I haven't seen the case, which is with HR, but I'm told that she felt uncomfortable when you introduced yourself."

"Are you kidding me?" I felt I was going to be sick on his desk. That could have been one way to touch him: put my lunch on his fresh pressed suit. I took a deep breath.

"The case is with HR now," he said. "Maria Duran is handling your file. She's also looking into your claims that your fellow workers' actions have hindered your performance."

"What does that mean specifically?"

"Well, if there were any fraudulent cases, she's trying to understand how this would have specifically affected you. She's also looking into your claim to have had your notary stamp stolen. Do you have any proof of that?"

"I sent you the police report."

He smirked. "I think you need to start thinking about substantiating some of the outrageous claims you've made over the last few months. I know the position has a lot of pressure, and…" but I was out of my seat at this point. I could see where he was going with this.

"I sent you every file I ever found to be fraudulent. There were hundreds of them."

He said nothing. And so I said: "What do you call a loan given to a company with bogus tax IDs and no earnings to repay that's charged off within six months, or a business that doesn't exist but yet pumps three million a week?"

But he wasn't listening to me. He was looking at my hands. I had them balled into fists. When I saw his reaction, I relaxed and took a breath. I knew I was shaking, but if he misinterpreted my frustrations as a threat to him, then it would really all be over. It would be too easy for them then. They would just paint me as some kind of deranged and disgruntled employee. We were fighting over my image at this point. They were already trying to say that I was incompetent and sexually inappropriate; if they could add violence to my list of offenses, then they would have the trinity. What kind of a company would ever hold on to an employee who was incompetent, sexually inappropriate, and violent? Not a bank with a reputation to keep.

I knew what was going on. I had been coached by the best. I had been inside other companies that underwent this same process on a smaller scale, and saw from the outside what it looked like when managers turned on employees who recognized their fraud. When you begin committing crimes, everyone who is not with you is against you. Janson knew this, and that was why he never did a thing about the fraud I turned in. He knew as well as I did what was going on. I showed him. He wasn't stupid. But he also wasn't going to go against the company tide, especially not for me.

Chapter 35

When I left Janson's office that day, I felt a mixture of anger and despair. I sat at my desk feeling lost while staring at my computer screen. I knew I couldn't remain inactive and that I had to do something. I considered writing up my letter of resignation, but I wouldn't give up that easily. I had to stick it out until the end. The bitter end. I would just endure.

In front of me on the desk, I had a file full of the fraud I had gathered since August. New cases continued to crop up. Interestingly enough, most of them had originated out of East Northport after Anjali left. I had been keeping this information to myself because I didn't want to add more fuel to the fire, but we were at an impasse now. If they were just going to wear me down by slowly eroding my resolve, then I couldn't remain motionless, especially if the decision to terminate me had already been made, which I knew it had. In that case I shouldn't bother trying not to rock the boat.

It was then that I resolved to turn in more of the fraud, and to go around Janson and directly to security once again. If Janson was going to ignore the fraud, maybe Esperanza wouldn't. I hadn't been turning these files in with the same regularity as before because it was meaningless, and it only seemed to hurt me more. Now I realized that I was giving them just what they wanted—silence. I thought it was time to create a reaction. Fraudulent accounts were still being opened. I had even found more accounts where the records indicated they had closed the day before they opened. What this meant in plain terms was that the bank was still duplicating its customers' identities in order to launder money.

I had also noticed something else that rekindled my determination to push back. While I had found more fraud coming out of HSBC branches, I had also seen that several of the Goldfarb accounts as well many of DeFipo's accounts had been closed. Several of the other business accounts, including S&S, had also been closed without a trace. Seeing that, I knew the bank was in the process of cleaning up the problem. These were all accounts I had reported. You would think I'd have gotten an award or at least a plaque and a thank you. But now that I had sat on all this new fraud for a while, and realized that the bank was just going to constrict around me, I resolved to start handing it in again. It was either go back to reporting the fraud or sit on my hands while they erased the records and then terminated me for "not meeting behavioral and performance expectations."

I attempted to arrange a meeting with Esperanza, but I couldn't get him on the phone. I waited a few days more and tried again. I left messages, but the head of security was not returning my phone calls. It was already November. I decided that since I couldn't get Esperanza, I would report some of the accounts to Janson. I had been entirely reluctant to see him about this because I knew it would become explosive. So when I walked into his office with a fresh batch of fraudulent accounts and questionable loans that day, I knew what I was getting into. I was prepared to stop, drop, and roll.

When I showed him the files, he lost his cool altogether.

"You fucking asshole. You just don't learn, do you?" He pushed the files back toward me over his desk. "This shit doesn't exist."

"Then what is it?"

"I've about had it with you, John."

"Then I guess we feel about the same way. Are you going to fire me for handing in a file full of fraud? You know as well as I do that if I showed that to anyone with a bank account they would know what they were looking at, Mitch."

"And who would you show that to, John?"

"I don't know, who should I show it to?"

"HR is handling this now, John."

"What's HR know about money laundering, Mitch?"

"Get out."

"Is it standard practice to have HR investigate money laundering?"

"I told you to get out of my office. I'll call security."

"Good, cause I can't seem to get them on the phone anymore."

We looked at each other for a few seconds without saying a word.

"I'm not going away with this shit," I said.

"Oh, but you're going to go away," he said.

"What's that mean? You threatening me?"

"Just get the fuck out of here."

I closed the door behind me and went to my desk. I picked up the phone and dialed Esperanza's number, partially out of desperation but mainly from a sense that I needed to have someone take note of what I'd found. He answered on the second ring. I told him that I continued to find more fraud from the same branches, and even though Anjali had been removed, new cases using the same pattern were appearing.

"I'd like to meet with you," I said.

"I don't think that'll be possible John."

"What do you mean?"

"I mean I've been told not to meet with you again. I'm only supposed to talk with you when you're at your desk from this number, and not from your cell phone."

"I need the fraud I've found to be on the record."

"It's on the record."

"Janson said they weren't able to substantiate my claims. It's nonsense, I know…"

"Don't talk to him anymore. Don't tell him anything. When you have fraud, send it to me."

"I've found some more stuff that's real strange. I've got to see you."

"Just let it go, John."

But I ignored what he said and started to tell him about the closed accounts. "I've also noticed that a number of the accounts I turned in for being fraudulent have been closed."

"Just let it go, John."

"But if they're actually closing accounts I handed in, it's proof that they know they were crooked. They can't at the same time say there was no fraud while they recognize there was by closing the accounts."

"I don't know anything about the accounts being closed right now, but just let it go, it's being handled."

"What?"

"You heard me. Let it go, John. It's not going to go anywhere."

"That's it?" I asked.

"That's it, John."

I hung up the phone and sat in silence at the desk. I couldn't take another day here. I felt like I was having a heart attack. In retelling the story, it's difficult to relay the real sense of despair I felt. When a bureaucracy aligns itself against you, their actions are subtle, but are nonetheless suffocating. And that's where I was right at that moment. I was suffocating.

Chapter 36

I felt like a dead man walking. But out of the blue Janson was getting demoted. After holding his position for only nine or ten months, it was like a slap in the face to him. I thought about stopping by his office to give him a corporate pep talk. I would have loved to tell him that his position was a very stressful one and that sometimes we don't always accomplish the goals we set out to accomplish but that I believed in his ability. Yet I refrained from insulting him directly or in gloating at his loss, even though I wanted to. I wanted to be the better person. After hearing about his demotion, I somehow blamed him less for how he treated me. I think that was his way of protecting himself. He did still hold some power over me, and he could make my life more miserable than it needed to be. And to be truthful, it didn't need to be any more miserable than it was.

I was feeling deeply troubled because security would no longer accept any new cases of fraud from me. I was incredibly frustrated, especially when the accounts were closed suddenly overnight and also purged from the system. My sleep was disturbed. I tossed and turned, and when I did sleep it was so lightly that it was not refreshing. Then, I'd have trouble getting out of bed in the morning. I had never had trouble either sleeping (not since living in the trailer) or getting out of bed. When I did rouse myself, I'd think, "Why did I get up at all?" I didn't know what I went to work for. I went to a place everyday where I was a pariah. I couldn't get management or security or the authorities to do anything about the crimes I had seen, and I knew it was just a matter of time before I would be terminated. My one comfort was that I had saved everything. I had taped conversations, digital files, and paper files of crooked accounts by the basketful.

I also had the satisfaction of knowing that my coworkers still respected me. Several even understood what had happened and empathized with the position I was put in. I wasn't a whistle-blower by nature. The bank made me have to become one. I don't care much for the term, but I would rather be that than allow myself to be ruined by them.

When Janson's replacement was chosen, I didn't expect anything to change. I went to see him a few days after he settled into the office in Melville, and introduced myself.

"Hello, Mr. Howard."

"Call me Ben."

The first-name basis thing is always disarming. His job is to supervise you, guide you, tell you what to do, and if he's just good old Ben he can't be all that bad.

Now a guy who makes you call him mister, he's uptight and full of himself; he's probably a tough guy. Do we want a friendly leader or a formal boss? Is one or the other more or less phony? So here we are starting out on an even and friendly basis. After the brief introduction I asked him, "Ben, do you mind if I tape record our conversation?"

"I don't mind; anything I say to you can be a matter of record."

Then I proceeded to ask him what he was going to do about the continuing fraud I found in multiple branches at HSBC. He looked at me coolly. We weren't buddies anymore, and he said, "I don't anticipate changing Janson's policy with regard to either these matters or to you."

"What about any new cases of fraud that I find?"

"They're none of your business, John. Plain and simple."

"And what about the fact that all the accounts that were formerly laundering money are now being closed overnight?"

"Again, it's none of your business."

I nodded to him and left his office. What was there to say? He might as well have been Janson. I would make no headway there. If he was really following Janson, then I was out, and he was going to be the one to give me that last shove.

Chapter 37

Not long after the arrival of my new best friend, Ben, I got a call from Maria Duran in HR. She wanted to arrange a meeting with me along with Ben. I suppose she wanted a witness; meetings with HR are always two on one. I went along with protocol, eager to see where this wide and windy path would lead me.

I sat down in her office. She didn't smile at me. I felt as if she were acting when she spoke, as if this were just a stoic role she was playing and a mask she had on.

"I want you to know that I am truly disgusted by your behavior. You have sexually harassed a fellow employee. When you met her behind the counter at East Northport on or about the date of June the fifth, you shook her hand in a totally inappropriate way. She felt uncomfortable with how you touched her. I am truly disgusted by this, Mr. Cruz. But as she is no longer an employee anymore and she has chosen not to press charges with the Suffolk County Police, it is HSBC policy not to take the matter any further. Do you have anything you'd like to add?"

I shook my head no. Ben sat beside me. He was watching like I was an interesting experiment. But this was just a formality I had to accept at this point. If I got angry or became belligerent or nasty, chances were good that they would send for security. I was, after all, a harasser. My handshake was now an offense to women. But I didn't want to remain totally silent either.

"You do know that the woman who charged me was Anjali's cousin."

Maria looked at me blank faced for a few moments, and then she said, "And Anjali is the woman you've accused of stealing your notary stamp?"

"As well as committing massive fraud and money laundering. Don't you find that a bit coincidental?"

But then she went on to a new topic.

"I have been reviewing the incidences which you have repeatedly brought to the bank's attention. My comments will be better summed up in the e-mail I am sending around to you and the other interested parties. But let me sum it up by saying, Mr. Cruz…"

I was now Mr. Cruz, but they were just Maria and Ben. Two regular people having to deal with someone unsavory. If they continued to treat me in this way, I might actually start to act as such. She went on: "We really expect that if you're going to make claims like you have that you back them up with evidence. Now, you say that former East Northport branch manager Anjali Indira duplicated your stamp, but you offer no proof that this is true."

"The proof is on a loan document which I never signed."

"Why didn't you bring this to my attention?"

"I had no idea who you were until very recently, and then I only thought you were handling this sexual harassment charge. All the paperwork regarding any claim I ever made was documented and handed over to either Mitchell Janson or the head of security, Steve Esperanza."

"It's incumbent upon you to provide the documents to the human relations personnel who are handling your case."

"What case?"

"You have alleged that there have been fraudulent activities taking place at HSBC bank, and that branch managers and executive vice presidents knew that it was occurring. These are very serious charges, Mr. Cruz."

"And I took them seriously; that's why I handed them all in."

"But you didn't think to bring this up with HR?"

"Do you have a lot experience investigating bank fraud, Ms. Duran?"

"I don't see why that's relevant."

"Why wouldn't it be relevant? But that's beside the point; it doesn't say anywhere that employees must send instances of fraud they discover to HR. That would be crazy. I followed the protocol and pushed it up the chain; I even contacted security."

"Your job performance has also slipped to an unsupportable level, Mr. Cruz. You were given several warnings to increase your book, but your numbers have continued to fall."

"It's difficult to maintain the same levels at a branch that had so many fraudulent accounts. Would you rather that I ignore money laundering when I find it? Is that the policy of HR regarding these sorts of crimes?"

"No one said that."

"Ben did."

Then Ben said: "What do you mean? I never told you anything of the sort! I would never tell an SBRM to ignore what he thinks is fraud."

"You did; in fact, I have a recording of you saying that just the other day."

"You recorded one of your managers." Maria now sat back in her chair and took a note on a piece of paper to her right. She looked incredibly disappointed with me.

"I can play it back for you if you want."

"It's against company policy to tape-record any HSBC employee at anytime."

"I asked for Ben's permission."

HSBC policy actually states that if the other person agrees to be recorded then it is OK to record.

"That doesn't matter." She said this as if I had broken one of the Ten Commandments, or as if I had broken all the commandments at once and even smashed the stone tablets they were written on.

After a long and awkward pause, Maria spoke up again: "And, Mr. Cruz, the fact that you see some accounts being closed from your end does not mean that those accounts were engaged in any type of extralegal behavior whatsoever. There are many reasons why they would be closed."

"Who told you I said that?" I asked. She said nothing. I said, "But don't you think it's funny, Maria, that all the accounts I pointed out as being blatantly fraudulent were closed?"

"The fact that accounts you brought to our attention have been closed is not evidence of wrongdoing."

"But if you know I brought them to your attention, then why do you say I never substantiated any of my claims? It sounds like fairly sound substantiation to me."

"That's enough, John," Ben said.

"I think this meeting is over," Maria said.

I just sat back thinking, "They don't know who or what I recorded on dozens of tapes. They don't know the amount of documents I have gathered. Maybe someday they will."

Chapter 38

On February the twelfth, I received my termination papers. The reasons they gave were that I had not maintained the level of performance expected of me, I had made unsubstantiated claims, and that I had tape-recorded bank personnel. The real reason was that I would not remain silent. I had discovered money laundering on a large scale in multiple locations and many accounts in an organized fashion, and a bank like HSBC could never let a charge like that stick, especially when they were ready, willing, and able to pay the fines so that the charges were dropped.

I discovered how the laundering of money works in the United States, and how the government and the major banks work to cover it up. When the public hears that a major bank must pay a fine for some infraction or multiple infractions, the assumption is that the fine is a penalty and that justice has been served. The truth is that the fine is not even a slap on the wrist. The fine is simply the cost of doing business, and though embarrassing in many respects, banks will make the payments and avoid both prosecution and the open airing of their books. They are the keepers of secrets. But those secrets can and do destroy regular working people. Had I not been experienced in dealing with bank fraud and attempted cover-ups, or if I had been new to the business of banking, I would never have known how to protect and defend myself against the criminals in the business. And if I had not kept a record, sometimes against company policy, of what certain branch managers and a senior VP had been doing, then I would have nothing to stand on now. Had I not seen firsthand what happens to those who point out corruption, then I might not have taken the measures I did to protect myself from the smear campaign they leveled against me.

On the other hand, had my introduction to banking been at HSBC under these circumstances, I might never have learned enough about the right way to do business. Fortunately, I had learned the old-fashioned idea of honest banking from one man, whom I hold out as one of the legends of the industry. He had raised me up to work in a straight and honest line, and I didn't know any other way to be. And prior to my introduction to baking under Lou, I had lived on the farm under another honest man, who took me in out of the goodness of his heart, simply because he believed it was the right thing to do. He hadn't raised me to be a crook, nor had he taught me to stand by when others were committing crimes. That's why he took me in in the first place.

If everyone simply remained silent in the face of corruption and theft, then corruption and theft would go unchecked. And if we can learn anything from the latest economic bubble burst, it's that what people do inside major companies really does matter. When dishonest cultures become ensconced, it's only a matter of time before the bloated waste brings down the whole system. And this is true whether it's a family, a small company, a corporation, or a country. The behavior of people matters.

I built a career and a family out of hard work, honesty, and dedication, and one goliath international bank with a habit of breaking the law decided that I was in its way. It dealt with me by destroying my career, and doing its best to paint me as an incompetent employee who was "crazy" and in over his head. I found myself in a position where I had to accept other people's abuse and criminal actions, or lose my job. But I wouldn't accept their actions. And I did my best to document what they had done, and what they were doing to me. I refused to be a part of their crimes, and I have written this book as my redemption.

While neither the company, security, the auditors, nor the DA listened, I believe that people will listen. They deserve to hear this story. I do not believe that I stood alone, or that what I did was for nothing. I still believe in the light at the end of the tunnel. I believe that good will always prevail over evil in the long run. And I know that if doing the right thing doesn't start with one person, it won't start anywhere.

Made in the USA
Lexington, KY
02 February 2012